CREATING A STRESS-FREE OFFICE

Creating a Stress-free Office

SIMON PRIEST and JIM WELCH

Illustrations by William Parsons

Gower Management Workbooks

Published by
Gower Publishing Limited
Gower House
Croft Road
Aldershot
Hampshire GU11 3HR
England

Gower
Old Post Road
Brookfield
Vermont 05036
USA

ISBN 0 566 07973 9

British Library Cataloguing in Publication Data
Priest, Simon
  Creating a stress-free office. – (Gower management workbooks)
  1. Job stress 2. Stress management
  I. Title II. Welch, Jim
  158.7'2

Typeset in Melior by Wileman Design and printed in Great Britain by MPG Books Limited, Bodmin.

Contents

PART III   WHAT ARE THE SYMPTOMS OF STRESS?

HOW TO GET THE MOST FROM THIS WORKBOOK

This book is about
This book is about managing stress in organizations. Too many people still regard stress as an issue for individuals to manage alone. The authors start from the premise that stress is damaging to the organization as a whole and that great mutual benefit is to be gained by working on it together.

Furthermore it is argued that effective stress prevention can only happen if teams collaborate together to understand stress, audit its causes and symptoms and then act to deal with the total impact.

This Workbook explains what the law says about the responsibilities of the organization in controlling stress. It shows how managers can develop practical strategies to reduce or prevent stress occurring within their teams. It reveals that inoculating your staff against stress is a powerful management skill which can be employed to improve the well-being and performance of people within your organization.

This book will enable you to achieve
On completing Part I you will be clear what stress is and you will understand the responsibilities of your organization under the law.

On completing Part II you will be able to state the particular causes of stress within your team and develop strategies for reducing their impact.

On completing Part III you will learn how to recognize the symptoms of stress in your team and understand what role you have to play in supporting individuals.

On completing Part IV you will understand the four main strands applicable to stress reduction and how to apply them in your workplace.

How to work through this book

It is important to recognize that the messages in this Workbook can apply to your personal life as well as your professional life.

Work through the material systematically and in the order in which it is set out if you are to get maximum value from the exercises. Make sure that you complete each activity before moving on to the next unit of work. The Group Activities and Tips, however, are likely to be applied over the longer term.

THE SECRETS OF SUCCESSFUL MANAGEMENT

If you are reading this book it is probably because you want to be a more effective manager. But what exactly is an effective manager? What is it that effective managers do that others do not? When people say that their manager is outstanding, what is it about them, their systems and their behaviours that make them so outstanding?

We would like you to reflect on those questions for a few minutes.

Suppose that a prestigious publisher has come to you and said that you have been identified by your organization as one of their outstanding managers. They are not sure how you do it but you seem to have the gift of getting everyone in your team to perform at the very peak of their potential.

The publisher wants you to write a book sharing your secrets of success with the world. The first thing you do is to sit down and brainstorm what are the hallmarks of a great manager and team player.

Think about all the ways you try to be a good manager. Draw on everything you have learnt so far from your observations of other managers as well as your experience of the management development programmes you have participated in.

What is Stress?

Learning Objectives

Part I will enable you to:

- state what the effect of stress is on organizations and what the law says about your responsibilities
- state what stress is
- explain the implications of the above for you as a manager.

Learning Areas

In this unit you will:

- identify your secrets of successful management in the context of inoculating your team against stress
- understand the facts relating to stress and what the law says
- decide what your organization needs to do.

Exercise 1: The secrets of successful management

Use the diagram below to write down your ideas in single words or short phrases. Do not spend more than three or four minutes on this.

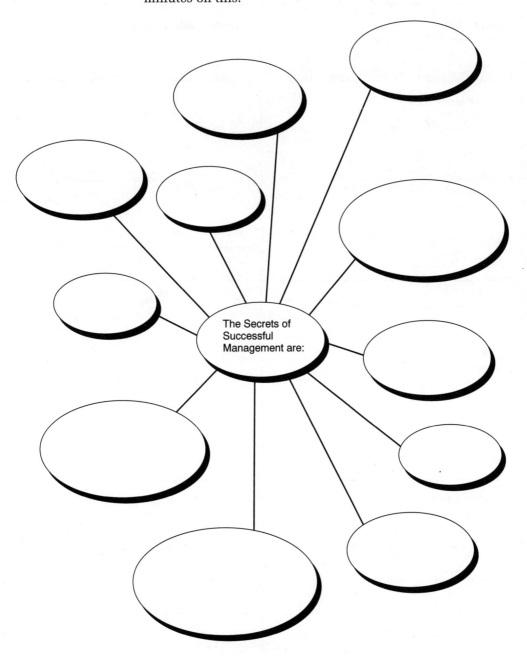

The Secrets of
Successful
Management are:

CHAPTER HEADINGS

Your next task is to group the ideas you have just produced and decide on a maximum of six chapter headings for your book.

Chapter Title	Chapter Sub-headings
1. _____	_____
	_____
	_____
2. _____	_____
	_____
	_____
3. _____	_____
	_____
	_____
4. _____	_____
	_____
	_____
5. _____	_____
	_____
	_____
6. _____	_____
	_____
	_____

SKILLBUILDER

ANSWER
BOX

You have probably decided on headings connected with the following issues:

- leadership and motivation
- communicating and listening
- interpersonal skills
- setting objectives and defining the vision
- coaching and supporting
- performance management
- setting priorities and good time management
- project management
- team building.

There is no set of absolutes which have to be in a book entitled 'The Secrets of Successful Management'.

However, we would like to suggest one more chapter heading for your book. The heading is 'Stress Inoculation'. Successful managers find ways consciously or otherwise of preventing their staff from becoming stressed. They inoculate their staff against stress.

This book will show you how to become a stress inoculator.

SKILLBUILDER

Exercise 2: Our attitudes to stress

If you are to understand stress a useful starting point is to consider your attitudes to the subject.

- Read the nine subjective statements commonly made about stress
- Place the statement you agree with most strongly at the top by writing the letter in the top diamond
- Place the statement you most strongly disagree with at the bottom
- Place the others on the diamond ranking – those you agree with most being placed higher.

THE NINE STATEMENTS

The following statements are in no particular order:

Place statements you agree with most strongly at the top.

Place the statement you least agree with at the bottom.

1. Stress comes from the organization, not from the individual.
2. Most illnesses are exacerbated by stress and many are caused by it.
3. An effective organization cannot afford to employ workers who are prone to stress.
4. Stress is good for you and for the organization in sensible amounts.
5. Stress is inevitable in business today and it is unrealistic to think you can eradicate it.
6. If a manager sees staff members under stress the best course of action is to send them to see a doctor.
7. Difficulties at work are less stressful than domestic problems.
8. Active sport and healthy diet are the best antidotes to stress.
9. High absenteeism is a good measure of stress in an organization.

Now turn the page to see our comments.

SKILLBUILDER

10

ANSWER BOX	There are no right and wrong answers; however, we would make the following observations.

STATEMENT	ANSWER
1. **Stress comes from the organization not from the individual.**	In the past there has been predominant emphasis on the individual bearing the responsibility for their own well -being in terms of stress. We would suggest that, in the future, organizations will increasingly recognize ftheir role in reducing stressful pressures and their legal obligation to do so.
2. **Most illnesses are exacerbated by stress and many are caused by it.**	There are increasingly clear links between illness and stress which will be explored in Part III of this Workbook.
3. **An effective organization cannot afford to employ workers who are prone to stress.**	We would argue less that specific individuals are prone to stress, and argue more that specific situations are likely to lead to stress. Therefore effective organizations cannot afford to expose their workers to stressful situations.
4. **Stress is good for you and for the organization in sensible amounts.**	There is no doubt that all of us operate well under a certain amount of pressure.This is not the same thing as stress as will become clear in Part I, Unit 2 of this Workbook.
5. **Stress is inevitable in business today and it is unrealistic to think you can eradicate it.**	Modern life provides a diversity of ways in which it can cause us to feel stressed. As you read this book you will understand what they are, and you will also see that there is an equally wide range of actions you can take to reduce the causes of stress.
6. **If a manager sees staff members under stress the best course of action is to send them to see a doctor.**	This book is not intended to tell you how to treat the sufferer of stress. If there are worrying physical and emotional symptoms this is sound advice. However, this book will help you to prevent people becoming stressed in the first place.
7. **Difficulties at work are less stressful than domestic problems.**	It depends on your situation. Pressures at work and home exacerbate each other and conflict between the two can be a source of stress in itself.
8. **Active sport and healthy diet are the best antidotes to stress.**	They are certainly a very useful component in preventing you becoming stressed.
9. **High absenteeism is a good measure of stress in an organization.**	People are generally reluctant to cite stress as the cause of their absence but the link is well founded. Absenteeism rates will help you to audit stress in your organization intelligently but the building of a strong climate of trust in the team is the key to encouraging honesty about the stress people are experiencing.

SKILLBUILDER

GROUP ACTIVITY

The diamond ranking is an excellent and enjoyable activity to use with your team at a meeting or an away day. It will foster open discussion as well as raising the issue of stress.

Step 1 Preparation
- Enlarge the diamond ranking chart to A3 and make several copies
- Copy the nine statements and cut them up, putting the complete set into an envelope. Make several sets.

Step 2 Activity
- Divide your team into small groups of three or four
- Give each group one diamond ranking chart and one envelope containing the nine statements
- Give them the instructions that you have just followed for ranking them and tell each group that they all have to agree on the placing of each statement.

Step 3 Discussion
You will have to do very little talking during the discussion. The following questions will be enough to prompt people:

- What did your group put at the top?
- Why did you place it there?
- Did anyone else put that particular statement high up on their chart?
- What did other groups put at the top? Why?
- What did you put at the bottom? Why?
- Does their argument convince you to put that statement higher?

(This activity will take you a minimum of 30 minutes. The discussion will continue as long as you want it to!)

NOW COMPLETE THE FOLLOWING QUIZ GIVEN IN EXERCISE 3 (PAGE 13).
ALTERNATIVELY, YOU MAY TURN TO THE FAST TRACK SECTION ON PAGE 15.

Exercise 3: The facts about stress

QUIZ ON THE COST OF STRESS

There is a range of subjective perspectives surrounding the issue of stress. Increasingly research is starting to provide a clearer picture. Complete this simple Quiz and then turn to the Fast Track section on page 15 for the answers.

1. In rough terms we have 20 million workers in the UK, each working 200 days a year making a total of 4000 million working days.
   How many of these working days are lost through stress each year? _____
2. It may be assumed that an employer would be wary of employing someone they felt would be constantly absent for any reason.
   What percentage of employers say they would be unlikely to employ someone with mental health problems?

   _____
3. The British Safety Council studies all the causes of people taking time off work. Stress is in the top ten.
   What position would you place it in? _____
4. What percentage of sickness absences have a mental or emotional aspect to them? _____
5. Which of the following groups do you think suffer stress most in organizations?
   • Directors   _____
   • Senior Managers   _____
   • Middle Managers   _____
   • Administrative Staff _____
6. If there were no stress-related absences how much money would the whole country save? £_____
7. Apart from absenteeism, suggest three other ways stress could cost an organization money? _____

                                        _____

                                        _____

SKILLBUILDER

The facts about stress

If you wish, you may turn to page 13 for a Quiz on 'The facts about stress', to test how much you already know. Otherwise, read the following section.

STRESS LEADS TO LOST TIME

- According to information published by the British Safety Council, stress-related disorders lead to 90 million lost working days per year. The HMSO publication 'Understanding Stress' puts it lower at 40 million.
- The taboos surrounding mental illness mitigate against openness and honesty from those suffering stress. For example, The Psychiatric Bulletin 1995 reports that ignorance and stigmatism of people who have been mentally ill means that 28 per cent of employers say they would only occasionally, or never, employ them.

Note: There is now the Disability Discrimination Act 1995 which may be relevant.

STRESS CAUSES ILLNESS

- The second biggest category of occupational disease is stress caused or increased by work according to the British Safety Council. Back injuries constitute the largest category.
- Some estimates say that as much as 40 per cent of all sickness absence at work is attributable to some form of mental or emotional disturbance. Even a small reduction would therefore bring considerable financial benefit to an employer.
- Stress is experienced at low levels in organizations just as much, if not more, than at managerial and board level where people feel they have more control of their destiny.
- The term 'presenteeism' has been coined to describe employees at work who are unfit to be there or who work excessively long hours on a voluntary basis.

THE COST OF STRESS

- For obvious reasons the precise costing of the effects of lost time due to stress is difficult although a figure of £3000 million annually has been suggested (HMSO 'Understanding Stress'). Estimates which include NHS expenditure rise to £7000 million.

- A study of 700 Personnel and Human Resource Directors by the Industrial Society reported stress as causing:
  - decreased productivity
  - poor judgement
  - poor quality
  - poor customer care
  - high personnel turnover
  - low morale
  - increased accidents.

This is backed up by the Health in England survey conducted in 1996 with 4600 people which found that 69 per cent of women and 62 per cent of men had experienced moderate or large stress in the last year. The majority said that stress affected their work. This is corroborated by an Institute of Managers survey of 3000 managers, 90 per cent of whom said that stress was affecting the health and performance of employees.

People who cannot face work and become absentees can, in turn, create stress for their colleagues. Those people who do go to work find they have an increased workload because of absenteeism, and may be demotivated by the behaviour of their colleagues – the absentees.

Assessing the cost of stress

All of these costly problems are additional to people taking time off work. Now consider the following questions:

- How much does your organization rely on quality thinking, safe practices or any of the other areas listed above?
- How would you measure the cost of poor judgement in your organization?
- How would you measure the cost of poor behaviour in your organization?

The real cost of stress

It seems impossible to assess the real cost of stress. We know that a significant amount of time is lost through absenteeism. We can guess that the quality of work done by those who do not take time off is likely to reduce efficiency. We can be sure that there is a cost in terms of health care.

In addition to these tangible, if difficult to measure, costs is the personal burden that sufferers and their families experience. All of these costs add up to a serious problem which organizations and individuals avoid at their peril.

The law

You have looked at your own attitudes to stress and have seen some of the broad results of stress. Now look at what the law has to say on the subject.

The Case of *Walker* v. *Northumberland County Council*

John Walker worked for Northumberland County Council managing four teams of social workers in Blyth Valley. The pressure of work was increasing due to inadequate staffing for an increase in population and rapidly rising demands for social services especially in the area of child protection.

Walker was unable to persuade his superiors to take steps to reduce the pressure, for example by transferring workers from rural parts to Blyth Valley. Unable to cope with the ever-rising volume of stressful work, Walker suffered a nervous breakdown in November 1986.

He returned to work four months later telling his immediate superior that he would not be able to cope without support. This was provided on a daily basis in the form of a principal field work officer.

However, a backlog of work had developed; the support was soon withdrawn, and child care cases continued to increase. Within six months he could no longer cope and suffered another breakdown which left him unable to take on work of any responsibility ever again. John Walker was diagnosed as suffering from a 'stress-related anxiety state'.

At this stage Walker took action to claim damages against the Council for breach of duty of care as an employer in failing to take reasonable steps to avoid exposing him to a health-endangering workload. The argument was that the Council was aware of the situation. It was foreseeable and therefore the Council should have taken steps to alleviate it.

The judge found that in the case of the first breakdown the Council was not liable. However, in the case of the second breakdown he found in favour of Walker. The argument was that on his return to work the circumstances likely to result in another breakdown were quite foreseeable. The support which Walker would subsequently need was also quite clear. By failing to provide this support, Northumberland County Council could reasonably be expected to foresee the risk to mental health to which it was exposing Walker and it was therefore found to be liable.

Walker was awarded damages of approximately £175 000.

WHAT ARE EMPLOYERS LIABLE FOR UNDER THE LAW?

The Health and Safety at Work Act 1974

This Act places a general duty on employers to ensure the health, safety and welfare of employees whilst at work. The Act refers to the employer having a duty of care to employees. There is no specific reference to stress-related illnesses though the case of *Walker* v. *Northumberland County Council* has virtually included them. Legal opinion emphasizes that merely to suffer from 'stress' would be insufficient to substantiate a claim: a diagnosis of psychiatric illness is required.

There is complementary legislation from Europe in the Health and Safety at Work Regulations 1992 which imposes a duty on employers to make a suitable and sufficient assessment of the risks to the health and safety of their employees. Like the British legislation it does not specifically discuss stress but we can assume an implied duty to consider this aspect of working hazards under the provisions of risk assessment.

The Regulations state that every employer shall make a suitable and sufficient assessment of the risks to the health and safety of employees whilst they are at work. They also discuss health surveillance with emphasis on the physical health of employees, but again it may be implied that the mental health and well-being of employees should also be considered.

Stress at work was one of the top three health priorities for the Health and Safety Commission in its 1994/5 Plan of Work.

It is reasonable to assume that employers must accept that they have a duty to take appropriate steps to minimize any risks of causing health-threatening stress at work.

The Walker case does not say that any employee who suffers a breakdown as a result of stress can automatically prove the employer liable. It does say that if the stress caused was fore-seeable and still nothing was done by the employer then that employer may be found to be negligent and therefore liable.

As a result of the Walker case the Law Commission has

provisionally agreed that 'there should be liability where an employer has negligently overburdened its employee with work thereby foreseeably causing him or her to suffer psychiatric illness'. This is not the same as expecting employees to be protected from all pressure. The courts appreciate that some jobs have inherently and explicitly higher levels of demand.

The Employment Protection Act 1978

In addition to the Health and Safety legislation, under Section 55 (1) (c) of the Employment Protection (Consolidation) Act 1978 an employee may, in some circumstances, terminate a contract without notice due to an employer's conduct. The employee may also be entitled to claim constructive dismissal at a later date. In lay terms the employee would be arguing that they were effectively forced to resign by being subjected to unacceptable working conditions endangering their health.

Dr Chris Johnstone had worked, for a long period of time, an average of 100 hours per week as a junior doctor. Eventually he felt unable to continue and resigned. Later he claimed constructive dismissal, finally settling an action against Camden and Islington Health Authority for £5600 compensation (plus £150 000 legal costs).

In *Whitbread plc t/a Thresher* v. *Gulley* an inexperienced off-licence manager resigned after being transferred to a large branch with insufficient staff cover resulting in her having to work long hours. She was able to successfully claim unfair constructive dismissal and settle on damages which, like the case of Dr Chris Johnstone, were relatively low.

The Sex Discrimination Act 1975 and The Race Relations Act 1976

These Acts are relevant to the extent that unlawful discrimination leads to emotional distress. They forbid direct and indirect discrimination as well as racial and sexual harassment. Both constitute 'less favourable treatment' which is unlawful. It is usual for awards to include compensation for injury to feelings.

Sexual or racial harassment is particularly likely to lead to stress-related illnesses. A harassment claim may be directly against the behaviour of a manager or because of the employer's failure to address the problem in the workplace.

The Disability Discrimination Act 1995

It is not clear in this complicated legislation to what extent a stress-related illness may be regarded as a disability. If such an illness is termed a disability, it may prohibit employment selection practices which discriminate against people who have suffered from mental illness though the legal position is not at present resolved.

It is more certain, however, that employers must engage in fair procedures (for example, consultation, job modifications, flexibility) before dismissing an employee suffering from a stress-related illness.

Workplace bullying

This is being increasingly acknowledged in the 1990s to the extent that one-third of current stress-related employment legal cases are estimated to be primarily attributable to workplace bullying. In the UK this legal action falls within one of the above statutes as, unlike Sweden and Norway, there is no generic anti-harassment legislation. Whilst individual cases of physical, sexual and racial intimidation in the Armed Forces and Police have achieved notoriety, surveys have confirmed substantial emotional abuse in a variety of workplaces. Trade Unions in the National Health Service, Teaching Unions and the Industrial Society, to name but a few, have held recent conferences on this problem. Complainants refer to corporate as well as individual bullying, often citing their immediate line-manager. Reasons include thoughtlessness, excessive business competition, 'passing on the pressure', deliberate attempts to force employees to leave without compensation and emotional instability. Recent research has even identified aggressive e-mail ('flame mail') as being a surprisingly common source of distress.

Many organizations now have 'equal opportunities' or 'dignity at work' policies.

WHAT ARE THE CONCLUSIONS?

It is important that high profile court cases do not set the precedent for all future approaches to stress in organizations with battle lines drawn in a confrontation between employers and their employees.

Where an organization fails to protect a worker from damaging stress no one wins. The settlement given to Walker could be argued to be poor compensation for a career ruined and personal well-being destroyed. The County Council not only paid out a large settlement but spent considerable time and resources in fighting the case and trying to protect its good name.

It would have been more desirable for Walker, for the County Council, for other council workers and for the rate payers of Northumberland if the issue had been effectively addressed before it became a crisis. This is equally true for racial or sexual harassment, and other forms of workplace bullying.

YOU MAY NOW CONTINUE WITH THE SKILLBUILDER EXERCISE ON PAGE 23 ,
OR MOVE TO THE NEXT FAST TRACK SECTION ON PAGE 25.

21

Exercise 4: What is your organization doing?

On the table below list in general terms what your organization is doing to tackle the issue of stress.

What your organization is doing	What your organization should be doing

Now turn the page to see what we suggest.

SKILLBUILDER

ANSWER BOX

This Workbook contains detailed practical strategies to tackle stress. We would suggest, however, that there are some general starting points for any organization which is serious about addressing the issue.

- **Health surveillance** of employees (including being alert to personal distress, absenteeism, increased use of alcohol and other symptoms of stress).
- **Monitoring** of increased levels of work required of employees.
- **Auditing** and understanding the possible sources of stress within the organization.
- **Practical actions** taken to minimize stress where it occurs such as providing job variety, support to alleviate excessive workloads and personal stress management programmes.
- **Raising awareness** of the issues amongst managers in the organization.

Compare our suggested answers with your own list on page 23.

- Is there anything your organization is not doing?
- What should you think of starting to do?
- What actions can you personally take to start this process?

YOU MAY NOW CONTINUE WITH THE SKILLBUILDER EXERCISE AT THE BEGINNING OF UNIT 2 (PAGE 29) OR MOVE TO THE NEXT FAST TRACK SECTION ON PAGE 25.

Stress inoculation – an additional 'secret'

If you have completed the exercise 'The secrets of successful management' from the Introduction to the Workbook, you will have produced a list of key management skills that are similar to the following:

- leadership and motivation
- communication and listening
- interpersonal skills
- setting objectives and defining vision
- coaching and supporting
- performance management
- setting priorities and good time management
- project management
- team building.

We would like to add another key skill to this list, stress inoculation, that is, the skill of *preventing your staff from becoming stressed.*

Stress inoculation is a tool of effective management alongside all the other management skills. It is a skill you can learn.

If you practise any management skill effectively then you will *at the same time* inoculate your staff against stress.

EXAMPLE: OBJECTIVE SETTING

- Objectives are agreed through consultation
- They are challenging but realistic
- You offer coaching and support to help staff achieve their objectives.

This is not a course in objective setting but if all managers followed the list above then they would find a reduction in the stress levels amongst their staff. You may of course be doing this already which would explain why objectives are not a source of stress in your team.

The consequences of failing to develop the skill of stress inoculation are extremely serious for your team, as the following two examples illustrate.

EXAMPLE 1: KEVIN

The MD reflected with satisfaction that motivation was rapidly becoming his strong suit

This cartoon illustrates the true story of Kevin, a supervisor in a large chemical company who had been given 106 objectives by his manager. Kevin told us, 'I've got time to do my job but I never have time to do my objectives. I just feel so stressed'.

EXAMPLE 2: MARK

Mark used to work for the sales arm of a computer company. He had very demanding sales targets set for him according to a company formula. If he was successful he could earn in excess of £100 000 per year but he always knew that the lowest performing 20 per cent were fired. He could never ask for help since the culture was one of 'every man for himself'. He left the job suffering severe symptoms of stress. He is now looking for another job.

YOU MAY NOW CONTINUE WITH THE SKILLBUILDER EXERCISE ON PAGE 29, OR MOVE TO THE NEXT FAST TRACK SECTION ON PAGE 31.

Learning Areas

In this unit you will:

- produce your definition of stress to compare with a psychologist's definition
- understand when pressure becomes stress
- start to analyze what causes stress in your team.

Exercise 5: What is stress?

In this unit we will begin to explore what stress is. First we would like you to complete the exercise below answering the question: 'What comes into your head when you think of the word "stress"?'

Write down as many ideas as you can in single words or short phrases.

A DEFINITION OF STRESS

Use some of the words and phrases to produce a definition of stress in no more than 25 words.

Stress is ...

A psychologist's definition of stress

Psychologists suggest a general definition of stress as follows:

> **'Stress is a feeling which results from excessive pressures and environmental stimulation'.**

Note that stress here is defined as a human reaction, not a feature of the environment.

By implication this feeling is unpleasant and unwanted, and there are likely to be associated medical symptoms if the pressure persists. There is a no single 'stress feeling'. For any individual it is a range of thoughts such as:

- 'I am failing'
- 'I can't cope'
- 'This isn't fair'
- 'Nobody cares'
- 'I can't switch off.'

It also involves a changing mixture of strong emotions such as:

- anger
- anxiety
- fear
- depression
- tension
- exhaustion
- despair
- isolation
- resentment.

The final element of stress will be a change in behaviour as the sufferer tries to do something about the situation or about the range of physiological, cognitive and emotional aspects of stress described above.

Look back to the list of words and phrases you produced in the Skillbuilder exercise on page 29. How many of those focus on feelings?

Of course it is important to note that if we are angry, for example, it does not necessarily mean we are stressed. Stress can best be thought of as an umbrella term for a changing combination of thoughts and feelings.

Ask your team of staff the same question we asked you: 'What comes into your head when you think of the word "stress"?'

Step 1 Ask them to spend 3 minutes writing individual answers to the question.

Step 2 Conduct a brainstorming session in answer to the same question. Write all the answers on a flip chart at the front.

Please follow the rules of brainstorming:

• Write all answers with no comment or discussion
• Record answers word for word
• Keep the brainstorm session short (5 minutes maximum).

Step 3 In groups of three ask them to try to construct a definition of what stress is and write it on a flip chart. Ask each group to read out what they have written and explain what they mean.

Allow time for a few minutes' discussion of any issues raised.

This activity will take about 30 minutes.

WHEN PRESSURE BECOMES STRESS

We will now look at some examples of pressure (environmental stimulation) and see how they can lead to powerful emotions and feelings.

Environmental stimulation can be described as anything that happens around us which triggers brain activity. The environmental stimulation may, on its own, not necessarily feel unpleasant but it will contribute towards the total pressure being experienced.

THE PRESSURE CURVE

Our individual ability to cope with a given pressure varies over time with our changing personal circumstances. There may be other pressures facing us; our health may be poor; or we may have lost some important support such as a friend moving away from the area.

Sometimes a single traumatic event can produce a strong stress reaction on its own known as post traumatic stress disorder.

This requires a different approach – since the sufferer has been catapulted into an extreme state of stress – starting with professional counselling. That is not the remit of this book.

For most of us, most of the time, stress manifests itself gradually and this is usefully represented in the diagram below.

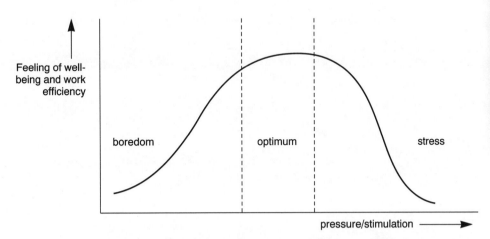

The horizontal axis represents increasing pressure on us while the vertical axis represents our increasing feelings of well-being and ability to perform to our full potential.

There is a widely accepted relationship between the pressure or stimulation acting on us and our feelings of well-being. As we tend to work best when we are feeling at our best the same relationship is true for our work efficiency.

For any given individual at any given time, for reasons discussed earlier, there is an optimum level of pressure or stimulation. This directly affects our overall level of brain activity known as cortical arousal.

If there is too little pressure or stimulation we eventfully perceive this as boredom and usually seek out activity. On the other hand, if the level of pressure is excessive for us and it is sustained this causes unpleasant levels of cortical arousal, negative emotions, physical symptoms and unhelpful thoughts.

This is the condition we know as stress.

YOU MAY NOW CONTINUE WITH THE SKILLBUILDER EXERCISE ON PAGE 35, OR MOVE TO THE NEXT FAST TRACK SECTION ON PAGE 41.

Exercise 6: Environmental stimulation and feelings

Read the descriptions of environmental stimulation (or pressure situations) and record what feelings you would expect to experience in these situations.

Do not treat each situation in isolation. We have provided a starting point where you are under-stimulated. From that point on, each new environmental stimulation comes on top of the ones before.

Environmental stimulation	Your feelings and emotions in response to the situation
1. Things are quiet at home and at work you have been in the same post for some years. You have your niche and your manager hasn't been asking much else of you for some time.	You feel rather uninspired. Confidence is only moderate. You are bored.
2. Your manager has demanded a report on your project for his meeting in one hour.	
3. You cannot get through to an important contact until this afternoon.	
4. You hear that you have been headhunted by a big multi-national who have heard great things about you and they want to meet you next week.	
5. Your partner gets flu.	
6. A colleague persuades you to do a parachute jump for charity. You will raise £10 000 but you have never jumped before and it is this weekend.	
7. Your daughter calls. She has forgotten her PE kit and she wants you to take it to school for her now.	
8. Your hard disk has crashed and you have lost a report which will take two days to rewrite.	
9. A close colleague is off ill and will not be in for three weeks. You have to pick up the pieces of a project you know will have been left in a mess.	

SKILLBUILDER

Environmental stimulation	Your feelings and emotions in response to the situation
10. Your section loses a large contract.	
11. The Managing Director wants you to give a presentation to the Board on a successful project you led last year.	
12. Your partner calls you to remind you that you are meeting old friends for dinner tonight and to make sure you are home early. You had forgotten.	

Most people doing this exercise, or experiencing something similar for real, find that often some of the pressure situations they are presented with seem like interesting challenges. Some of them have been actively sought out and welcomed. We are all likely to feel complimented by being headhunted, if a little nervous about the proposed meeting.

Even irritating hassles such as not getting through to that important contact are taken in your stride. However, as one pressure piles on top of another over time the resulting feelings become less pleasant and you may start to feel overwhelmed.

We would emphasize the following:
- Different events and situations can combine to constitute intolerable pressures.
- We are all unique. A situation perceived as full of pressure for one of us may appear relatively easy to cope with by someone else.
- Our individual ability to cope with a given pressure varies over time with our changing personal circumstances such as other pressures, health, mental well-being and availability of support.
- As important as the event/pressure itself is the psychological meaning we attach to it (as illustrated by the cartoon on the next page).

SKILLBUILDER

Gary took a moment to block out the niggling thought that a nation's hopes hung on the next few seconds. He spun round confidently and struck the ball ...

This point is further illustrated by the following examples.

EXAMPLE A: AN ORGANIZATION DECIDES TO UPGRADE ITS IT

The organization has conducted a major reappraisal of its IT systems. Whilst the change and the associated inconvenience are shared experiences across the organization, they are perceived in different ways.

Half the staff see the move as a vote of confidence in them and in the future prospects of the business. They feel excited and valued; after all, a lot of resources have been put their way. They are raring to go.

The other half resent the lack of consultation. They fear that they will not understand the new systems and, worst of all, they anticipate redundancies. A number of this group begin to experience stress.

EXAMPLE B: A NEW APPRAISAL SYSTEM IS INTRODUCED

The organization is trialling its new appraisal system which is more rigorous and time-consuming than the past system of annual reviews. Many of the employees welcome the new management interest and the guidance it provides. In particular they see the opportunity to talk with managers about their achievements and anticipate enhanced career prospects.

Others in the organization are confused with the process and cynical about the 'hidden agenda' of appraisal. They feel apprehensive about their appraisal interview and generally regard its introduction as a criticism of the workforce. They perceive lack of trust and belief in their professionalism. This group are more prone to stress.

NOW MOVE TO THE FAST TRACK SECTION AT THE START OF UNIT 3 ON PAGE 41.

37

Learning Areas

In this unit you will:

- draw your own pressure curve
- draw the pressure curve of colleagues
- plan actions to raise awareness within your team.

Personal pressure curves

The graphs below show three different pressure curves. Draw your pressure curve on the fourth graph.

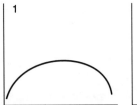 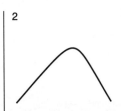 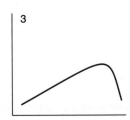 

WHAT SHAPE IS YOUR PRESSURE CURVE?

- Is it like the first one above with a wide area of tolerance indicating that you perform well under varying degrees of pressure?
- Is it like the second with a knife edge position which is a critical point that brings out the best in you?
- Is it like the third with a gradual build up and a definite point at which you go under rapidly?
- Or is it another shape?
- Mark your present position on the pressure curve.

It is useful to be aware of the totality of pressures acting upon us at work, at home and in our social life.

When we are at our optimum we may be over-optimistic or misjudge our capacity for additional pressure and we can slip into taking on too much all too easily. While we may be capable of operating under extreme pressure for short periods we are likely to experience stress if we are over-extended for too long.

To avoid this it is important to take on new tasks gradually and give ourselves time to step back from the high point on our curve by zealously protecting our personal time, particularly weekends and holidays.

YOU MAY NOW CONTINUE WITH THE SKILLBUILDER EXERCISE ON PAGE 43, OR MOVE TO THE NEXT FAST TRACK SECTION ON PAGE 51.

41

Exercise 7: The pressure curve of your team

- Try to draw the pressure curve of some of the people in your team
- Draw a collective curve for your team as a whole
- Mark on the line where you think individuals are at the moment
- List some of the specific pressures which face the team regularly
- Write these pressures along the horizontal axis.

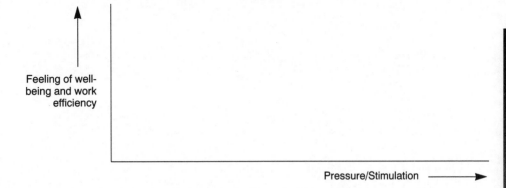

Feeling of well-being and work efficiency

Pressure/Stimulation

Parts II and III of this Workbook look at what causes stress and what the symptoms are so you may want to return to this exercise later.

NOW READ THE CHECK POINTS SECTION ON PAGE 45 TO REVIEW WHAT YOU HAVE
LEARNT FROM PART I OF THIS WORKBOOK.

43

SKILLBUILDER

Implications for managers

Review briefly what you have learnt in Part I of this Workbook about:

- The attitudes people have to stress
- The facts about the cost of stress to organizations
- What the law says about stress
- The differences in our responses to pressure situations
- The pressure curve.

What are the implications for you as a manager? What tangible actions can you take to start the process of getting your team and perhaps your organization to address the issue? Make a note of these below.

GROUP ACTIVITY

The following activities will complement suggestions for ways in which to discuss stress with colleagues made already in this Workbook.

Step 1

Draw a pressure curve on a flip chart. Explain the meaning of the horizontal and vertical axes and the notion that we all have an optimum point.

Step 2

Mark your own present position on the curve. Invite others in the team to do the same. Ask people to explain why they have placed themselves in the position that they have marked.

- What sort of challenges stimulate them to rise to the occasion?
- What sort of pressures accumulate to make them feel stressed?

Step 3

Discuss what you need to do as a whole team to make sure the levels of challenges and pressures are likely to help people stay at their optimum point on the curve.

The authors of this book see stress as a team issue. It is not something we can realistically expect people to deal with effectively in isolation at the point at which they have become stressed. It is an issue that the whole team should consider in order to prevent stress arising in the first place.

The first step is to identify what the causes of stress are in your organization and in your team. Identifying those sources of stress will require openness, honesty and strong relationships in your team. This is the subject of Part II of this Workbook.

What Causes Stress?

Learning Objectives

Part II will enable you to:

- identify the causes of stress within your team
- create an audit of what is causing stress to your team
- plan actions to reduce the impact of these factors.

Setbacks, Hassles and Challenges

Learning Areas

In this unit you will:

- understand how setbacks cause stress for individuals in your team
- understand how hassles cause stress for your team
- understand how challenges cause stress for individuals in your team.

Three categories of stress inducers

SETBACKS, HASSLES AND CHALLENGES

Part II of this Workbook is about helping you to identify what induces stress in your organization and in your team. So far we have described these inducers as events which produce feelings of pressure or stimulation. If these feelings grow out of proportion, then we are likely to experience stress.

It is useful to divide stress inducers into three broad categories. First, there are setbacks which are significant life events about which there is often little we can do. Examples of setbacks include serious illness to ourselves or those close to us, or redundancy.

Second, there are hassles. These are situations which we have not been proactive in bringing about and in many cases are ones we most definitely wish were not happening. These cover a wide range of situations from the hard disk on our computer 'crashing' to the organization announcing a far-reaching change programme.

Third, there are what we shall describe as challenges which are largely sought after or welcomed. An example might be an interview for a new, exciting and well paid job. It is something we have actively wanted but it is nevertheless going to put us into a situation which is full of pressure.

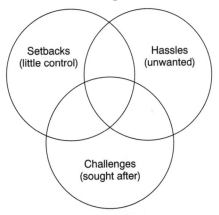

The diagram above is a helpful analytical tool bearing in mind the differences between individuals mentioned in Part I of this Workbook. When someone is feeling under pressure from a number of sources and therefore less able to cope, the challenge of that job interview may feel more like a severe hassle. The hassle of the announced change programme may be perceived as a major setback.

It can work the other way too. If you are feeling on top of things then the setback of sudden redundancy may become an exciting challenge of trying something new, especially if there is a good financial package with the new job.

The stress audit

The important first step in dealing with stress is to understand what is causing it in the first place. This process is called a stress audit. You will find popular stress audits in the pages of many magazines.

ARE YOU PUSHING YOURSELF TOO HARD?

The children were late for school, the computer won't print out that vital document and you haven't had time for lunch or to prepare for your performance review in ten minutes.

No wonder we get stressed out! But are you the type who soldiers on, always putting everyone else first?

James Pilkington, our resident psychologist, invites you to slow down for a moment and think about yourself. His practical stress audit will tell you whether you are simply 'Pushing Yourself Too Hard'.

1. I get headaches
a) Often   b) Rarely   c) Occasionally.

2. As a worker I feel I am a failure
a) Rarely or never   b) Sometimes   c) Often.

3. I get to sleep quickly and have a good night's rest
a) Rarely or never   b) Usually   c) Always.

4. I get attacks of giddiness and sickness
a) Hardly ever   b) Occasionally   c) Frequently.

5. I have recently changed job, moved house, got married, got divorced
a) All of the above   b) One or two of these   c) None.

6. I am angry with colleagues
a) Sometimes   b) Rarely or never   c) Most of the time.

7. I find concentrating and completing tasks
a) Usually very difficult   b) Sometimes difficult   c) Not difficult.

8. I tell other people how I am feeling
a) Rarely or never   b) Sometimes   c) Occasionally.

This stress audit has been adapted from a range of typical ones appearing in popular magazines.

What usually happens with stress audits such as the one above is that questions covering symptoms, events, stress inducers, perceptions and feelings are mixed together on a simple score chart. No attempt is made to differentiate between or to understand symptoms. There is no opportunity to examine the causes before results are given followed by a list of 'handy' tips for stress management.

Inevitably the tips apply only to what the reader can do individually such as to get more sleep, take up jogging or start thinking positively about him or herself. Undoubtedly some of the tips make sense but people reading them may feel unable to implement them. They are given little or no guidance on how to address the pressures arising from their working situation or how to prevent stress in the future.

Such approaches are simplistic. Minimal learning takes place and action is rare. They may also increase anxiety or feelings of helplessness.

CREATING A USEFUL STRESS AUDIT

If a stress audit is to have real value it should:

- carefully separate and analyse stress inducers and symptoms
- be relevant to our particular situation
- recognize the wide range of reactions to pressure
- be based on self-knowledge
- acknowledge our changing life circumstances
- identify existing good habits
- generate clear action plans
- emphasize the importance of helping each other.

The authors of this book cannot write a stress audit applicable to the situation of every reader. However, what we will do is invite you to create your own audit as you work through the rest of the programme.

Setbacks

THE HOLMES AND RAHE RESEARCH 1967

Holmes and Rahe wanted to investigate the relationship between stress and ill health. They interviewed a large sample of people about life events and linked these to their medical records.

While it is difficult to make generalizations about the stress levels any given life event is going to cause in a given individual, Holmes and Rahe were able to produce an estimate called the Social Readjustment Rating Scale.

Several thousand subjects were asked to attach a points rating to a range of life events. From their responses Holmes and Rahe constructed an index giving stress ratings from 1 to 100.

YOU MAY NOW CONTINUE WITH THE SKILLBUILDER EXERCISES ON THE FOLLOWING PAGES, OR MOVE TO THE NEXT FAST TRACK SECTION ON PAGE 61.

55

Exercise 8: Stress ratings of life events

Complete this activity before turning the page to look at the results of Holmes and Rahe's research.

Look at the life events listed below. Give each a score out of 100, where 1 represents a very low level of stress and 100 an unbearably high level of stress, according to the score you think they will have been given by the respondents in the Holmes and Rahe research. Rank the events in order of their score, highest score first.

LIFE EVENTS

- Personal injury or illness
- Retirement
- Foreclosure of mortgage or loan
- Sacked from job
- Son or daughter leaving home
- Change in financial state
- Jail term
- Change in the number of family get-togethers.

Your score	Your ranking	Life event	Actual score	Actual ranking
_____	1st	_____	_____	_____
_____	2nd	_____	_____	_____
_____	3rd	_____	_____	_____
_____	4th	_____	_____	_____
_____	5th	_____	_____	_____
_____	6th	_____	_____	_____
_____	7th	_____	_____	_____
_____	8th	_____	_____	_____

None of the life events listed above was given a score of 100 in the Holmes and Rahe stress rating. What do you think would get such a high score? What rating do you think winning £8 million on the National Lottery would bring?

Now turn to the next page to find out the actual rating for these events and read the complete Holmes and Rahe rating list.

SKILLBUILDER

Results of the Holmes and Rahe research

Ranking	Event	Score
1	Jail term	63
2	Personal injury or illness	53
3	Sacked from job	47
4	Retirement	45
5	Change in financial state	38
6	Foreclosure of mortgage or loan	30
7	Son or daughter leaving home	29
8	Change in the number of family get-togethers	15

The full Holmes and Rahe list is given below

Death of a spouse	100
Divorce	73
Marital separation	65
Jail term	63
Death of a close family member	63
Personal injury or illness	53
Marriage	50
Sacked from job	47
Marital reconciliation	45
Retirement	45
Change in health of family member	44
Pregnancy	40
Sex difficulties	39
Gain of a new family member	39
Business readjustment	39
Change in financial state	38
Death of a close friend	37
Change to a different line of work	36
Change in the number of arguments with spouse	35
Taking on a mortgage	31
Foreclosure of mortgage or loan	30
Change in responsibility at work	29
Son or daughter leaving home	29
Trouble with in-laws	29
Outstanding personal achievement	28
Wife begins or stops work	26
Children begin or end school	26

Change in living conditions	25
Revision of personal habits	24
Trouble with the boss	20
Change in work hours or conditions	20
Change in residence	20
Change in school	20
Change in recreation patterns	19
Change in social activities	18
Taking on a small mortgage or loan	17
Change in sleeping habits	16
Change in the number of family get-togethers	15
Change in eating habits	15
Holiday	13
Christmas	12
Minor violations of the law	11

Holmes and Rahe found that the two years prior to serious illness were often marked by a cluster of significant life events. They demonstrated that a high points score increased the statistical chances of becoming ill. They recommended therefore that two or more major life events in any one year should be avoided where possible.

Reference
Holmes, T.H. & Rahe, R.H. (1967), 'The Social Readjustment Rating Scale', *Journal of Psychosomatic Research*, **11**, 213–218.

SKILLBUILDER

Exercise 9(a): Setbacks

Take a look at Section One of the stress audit below. Record any examples of 'setbacks' that you are currently facing or have faced over the last 12 months. You may refer back to the Holmes and Rahe list on pages 58–9 to help you.

STRESS AUDIT – Part One: Inducers

SECTION ONE: SETBACKS

Make a list of the setbacks you are currently facing or have faced in the last 12 months.

_____

_____

_____

_____

_____

_____

_____

_____

_____

_____

_____

SKILLBUILDER

Hassles

The stress inducers we call hassles can be usefully subdivided into those connected with our environment and those connected to the culture we are working in.

ENVIRONMENTAL HASSLES

These are sources of stress which can be attributed to the working environment to some extent. They include the following factors.

Unfriendly physical features
- Heat and cold
- Insufficient light or excessive artificial light
- Noise – too loud, constant or unpleasant
- Smell – impure air
- Contamination – noxious chemicals
          – mud, dirt, oil, etc.

Internal physiological states
- Hunger and thirst
- Fatigue
- Illness
- Postural discomfort
- Boredom.

Social contact
- Crowding and lack of privacy
- Too frequent contact with others
- Over-emotional contact
- Loneliness.

Travel
- Distance to work
- Time spent on travel
- Frustration during the journey
- Discomfort on the journey
- Parking problems.

Information flow

Generally having to cope with too much information for the time available, for example:

- Excessive time watching a VDU
- Large numbers of e-mail messages
- Too many documents to read.

Work pattern

- Having to work at great pace
- Working long or unpredictable hours
- Unsocial hours
- Being 'on call' or being continually interrupted at work.

WORKING CULTURE – THE 8Cs

These are often people-orientated hassles which are more difficult to attribute. Successful organizations address these issues because they see them as impacting on the performance of their staff and therefore on the effectiveness and profitability of the organization. They include the following factors.

Change

- Particularly where we are not in control or not consulted
- Fear of the impact of the change on your life.

Conflict

- With your own conscience
- In interpersonal values, objectives and purposes
- An atmosphere of suspicion in the organization
- Perceived discrimination against certain groups
- Getting feedback only on poor performance
- Hostility or bullying.

Confusion

- Uncertainty in roles and status
- Lack of communication on organizational aims, objectives and progress
- Unclear limits of authority and responsibility
- Having to use unfamiliar technology.

Constraints

- Lack of skills or knowledge
- Lack of money, time and resources
- Lack of space in the workplace
- Lack of delegation or authority.

Constant demand

- Too many responses required
- Poor project planning or job design
- Unrealistic deadlines
- Too many people making demands of you.

Contractual worries

- Uncertain job prospects
- Short-term contracts
- Worries over pay and/or promotion.

Control

- The feeling that you have no influence
- Poor delegation practices
- Feeling helpless to change what is going wrong.

Career development

- Balancing private and professional life
- Child care arrangements and insufficient time spent with family
- Poor promotion prospects
- Low status
- Limited training opportunities
- Office politics.

SICK BUILDING SYNDROME

This is believed to result from a mixture of environmental and psychological hassles. Factors responsible include:

- poor air quality
- noise pollution
- inappropriate temperature
- sunlight deprivation
- some types of soft furnishings (particles)
- photocopiers and printers not separate and ventilated (gas and particles)

- general 'dehumanization' (harsh lighting, rows of computers)
- over-supervision (security cameras).

Between 20 and 30 per cent of offices built or refurbished in the last 20 years may be involved. These tend to be sealed for energy efficiency, multi-purpose and not responsive to the needs of individuals. Recent trends to reduce staff and premises overheads have compounded the problem.

Reported symptoms
These include:

- headaches and dizziness
- respiratory problems
- hearing and vision disturbances
- skin irritation
- lethargy and depression
- general feelings of stress.

Where commissioning a purpose-built design is too expensive or impractical, lesser changes have produced significant improvements. People generally prefer smaller groups sharing individual offices; with windows that open; and control over heating and lighting. Workplace design consultants advise that 'motorways' (main routes around the office), 'interaction hotspots' (social meeting places) and 'work clusters' (project working areas) should be carefully planned.

Many large companies pay careful attention to the interior design and external views, using pot plants, trees, artwork and water. Others use music and even smells to relax and stimulate but since this is centrally controlled it can be counter-productive.

YOU MAY NOW CONTINUE WITH THE SKILLBUILDER EXERCISES ON THE FOLLOWING PAGES, OR MOVE TO THE NEXT FAST TRACK SECTION ON PAGE 67.

Exercise 9(b): Hassles

Record in Section Two of your stress audit the hassles you regularly face in relation to your working environment, under the given headings.

STRESS AUDIT – Part One: Inducers

SECTION TWO: HASSLES

Environmental hassles
List the hassles you regularly face in relation to your working environment under the given headings.

Unfriendly physical features _____

_____

Internal physiological states _____

_____

Social contact _____

_____

Travel _____

_____

Information flow _____

_____

Work pattern _____

_____

Now record the level of pressure created by the cultural hassles you face. Mark the level (high, medium or low) for each issue and create your own graph by linking the points.

Cultural hassles
Record level of pressure created by the cultural hassles you face.

High

Medium

Low

Change Conflict Confusion Constraints Constant demand Contractual worries Control Career development

---

Exercise 9(c): Hassles for other occupations

Complete a stress audit similar to the one you have just done for yourself for a sample of other occupations. Although you may not be familiar with these occupations try to identify **one** environmental hassle under each heading.

Draw the likely shape of the graph of cultural hassles for each group using a different colour pen for each profession.

Do the same for the profession of a friend or partner.

Environmental hassles

List hassles these professionals would face in the working environment.

	Nurse	Police officer	Football manager	Your partner or friend
Unfriendly physical features				
Internal physiological states				
Social contact				
Travel				
Information flow				
Work pattern				

Cultural hassles

Record level of pressure created by cultural hassles.

High

Medium

Low

Change · Conflict · Confusion · Constraints · Constant demand · Contractual worries · Control · Career development

Key: Nurse – blue; Police officer – black; Football manager – red; Other – green.

NOW MOVE TO THE FAST TRACK SECTION ON THE FOLLOWING PAGE.

Challenges

The challenges in our lives are generally sought after and welcomed. In order to understand challenges it is useful to clarify the different aspects by asking four questions. These are detailed below.

To what extent is it an emotional challenge?
- Involving close personal relationships
- Presenting yourself to new people in new situations
- Forming and reforming relationships at work.

Is there a physical element to this challenge?
- Short-term challenges pushing us to our limits
- Long-term demands on our staying power
- Substantial travel.

Is it an intellectual challenge?
- Stretching our mental capabilities
- Learning new skills
- Coping with large amounts of information.

What meaning does the challenge have for us?
- Another routine project
- A critical step towards promotion
- A chance to make up for past mistakes
- An opportunity to prove a point to ourselves or others
- An important expression of our personal value system.

YOU MAY NOW CONTINUE WITH THE SKILLBUILDER EXERCISES ON THE FOLLOWING PAGES, OR MOVE TO THE NEXT FAST TRACK SECTION ON PAGE 77.

67

Exercise 10(a): Analysing challenges

Choose one of the case studies below and, by answering the questions in the matrix, analyze the nature of the challenge.

Case Study X

Susan is a project manager with a large computer systems organization. She has been chosen ahead of some more obvious candidates to lead a large project team to develop an important bid to win a major contract with the Department of Trade and Industry to install new IT systems.

There are members of the team she doesn't know well but she does know there has been some competitive antagonism in the past between some of the group members. Susan has a strong track record in project planning and motivating teams to pull together.

She is much less knowledgeable on the cutting edge technology which will be needed to win the bid but prides herself on being able to learn fast.

The client's offices are spread countrywide and there will be key presentations to make at regular intervals during the process as the numbers of bidders are gradually cut down.

If this project is successful it will make Susan's name in the company. It is possible she could achieve her ambition to become the first female director.

Case Study Y

Helen used to work as an operator in a glass factory five years ago. Since then she has taken time off to have twins. They are now at primary school where she has become involved in the Parent/Teacher Association (PTA).

The other parents active in the PTA seem to her to be more articulate and able. A number of them have important jobs. Helen's own confidence has been on the wane. People always seem to be asking her when she is going back to work.

Helen has been encouraged to take on the organization of the summer fete at the school following the angry departure of another parent who rubbed everyone up the wrong way including the headteacher.

Helen knows she will have to organize the other parents to run various stalls and activities. There are lots of things she has no idea about including where to get gas to fill the helium balloons and what, if anything, she needs to inform the local police about. The parent who has left the PTA knows all of this. Helen would desperately like to get her involved. She hates animosity.

On top of all this her husband says she is crazy to take it on.

To what extent is it an emotional challenge?	Is there a physical element to this challenge?
•	•
•	•
•	•
Is it an intellectual challenge?	What meaning does the challenge have?
•	•
•	•
•	•

As important as the event/pressure itself is the psychological meaning we attach to it.

Now select a challenge that **you** have faced in the past. Use the matrix of questions below to produce one statement in each box which describes why the challenge produced pressure for you.

The Challenge	
To what extent was it an emotional challenge?	Was there a physical element to the challenge?
Was it an intellectual challenge?	What meaning did the challenge have for me?

Exercise 10(b): Assessing your challenges

You are now ready to complete the final section in Part One of your stress audit.

- List the major challenges you have faced over the last 12 months
- Assess your current situation in terms of the pressure you are under from setbacks, hassles and challenges. Place yourself on the continuum line.

STRESS AUDIT – Part One: Inducers

SECTION THREE: CHALLENGES

Challenges _____   _____

_____   _____

_____   _____

Overall pressure level
Position yourself on the continuum line below taking into account all the setbacks, hassles and challenges you are facing. We suggest you return to this three or four times over a couple of days to produce an average estimate.

Too low	Low	Optimal	High	Too high

Now, on the next two pages, combine the first three sections of Part One of your stress audit to get a complete picture of stress inducers.

STRESS AUDIT – Part One: Inducers

SECTION ONE: SETBACKS

Make a list of the setbacks you are currently facing or have faced in the last 12 months.

_____

_____

_____

_____

_____

_____

_____

_____

_____

_____

SECTION TWO: HASSLES

Environmental hassles

List the hassles you regularly face in relation to your working environment under the given headings.

Unfriendly physical features   _____

_____

Internal physiological states   _____

_____

Social contact   _____

_____

Travel   _____

_____

Information flow   _____

_____

Work pattern   _____

_____

Now record the level of pressure created by the cultural hassles you face.
Mark the level (high, medium or low) for each issue and create your own graph
by linking the points.

Cultural hassles
Record level of pressure created by the cultural hassles you face.

High

Medium

Low

| Change | Conflict | Confusion | Constraints | Constant demand | Contractual worries | Control | Career development |

SECTION THREE: CHALLENGES

Challenges _____   _____

_____   _____

_____   _____

Overall pressure level
Position yourself on the continuum line below taking into account all the
setbacks, hassles and challenges you are facing. We suggest you return to
this three or four times over a couple of days to produce an average estimate.

| Too low | Low | Optimal | High | Too high |

NOW MOVE TO THE FAST TRACK SECTION AT THE START OF UNIT 2 (PAGE 77).

SKILLBUILDER

Learning Areas

In this unit you will:

- review setbacks, hassles and challenges
- create an audit of the causes of stress in your team
- generate questions to help you in identifying what is causing stress for the team.

Identifying setbacks, hassles and challenges

Let us look again at the definitions of the three categories of stress inducers.

Setbacks

Setbacks are essentially life events over which we feel we have little control such as illness or redundancy. These may also include milestones such as marriage or retirement.

Hassles

Hassles are largely unwanted and often less obvious to us than the challenges. They include pressures produced by our day-to-day environment such as our working conditions and travel arrangements.

Hassles also include more substantial pressures produced by the culture in which we work such as the constancy of demand made on us, the resource constraints and the level of control we have in our work.

Challenges

Challenges are situations which are likely to produce pressure for us but which, nevertheless, we have actively sought or at least we welcome them once they appear to some extent.

They normally have an emotional, physical and intellectual element to them. A challenge will also have a unique psychological meaning for us which may make it exciting but also adds to the potential for stress.

YOU MAY NOW CONTINUE WITH THE SKILLBUILDER EXERCISES ON THE FOLLOWING PAGES, OR MOVE TO THE NEXT FAST TRACK SECTION ON PAGE 85.

77

Exercise 11: Pressure situations

Read the following list of pressure situations and decide which
you would describe as setbacks, which as hassles and which as
challenges.

1. Having to take on the work of an ill colleague
2. Chairing an important meeting
3. Breaking your ankle
4. Speaking on local radio
5. Buying a new car
6. Having to spend Christmas away from the family
7. Your child leaving home for university at 17
8. Cooking for a dinner party for eight friends
9. The neighbour's dog barking continuously
10. Playing the lead role in your amateur dramatic group
11. Unexpectedly heavy traffic
12. Organizing a children's party
13. Changing to a different line of work
14. Moving house after a fire
15. Working in a crowded office with lots of unpleasant banter
16. Office heating breaking down
17. Having to work late at the last minute.

Write them in on the diagram below placing the situations
which you think would produce a high level of pressure at the
top of each circle and situations of less pressure at the bottom.

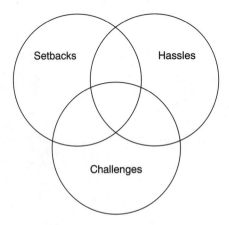

NOW TURN THE PAGE TO READ OUR INTERPRETATION OF THESE SITUATIONS.

ANSWER BOX

The categories we would normally put them into are listed below. However, our interpretation depends on our current state of mind, particular personal circumstances and the present level of environmental stimulation to which we are subjected. When we are feeling under pressure, challenges and hassles are more likely to be seen as setbacks, whereas when we are 'coping' we are more inclined to view events as challenges. Compare your categorization with the one below and where they are different check your rationale.

Setbacks

Changing to a different line of work
Having to spend Christmas away from the family
Your child leaving home for university at 17
Moving house after a fire
Breaking your ankle.

Hassles

The neighbour's dog barking continuously
Having to work late at the last minute
Working in a crowded office with lots of unpleasant banter
Having to take on the work of an ill colleague
Unexpectedly heavy traffic
Office heating breaking down.

Challenges

Chairing an important meeting
Speaking on local radio
Buying a new car
Cooking for a dinner party for eight friends
Playing the lead role in your amateur dramatic group
Organizing a children's party.

It gradually dawned on Pauline that what had seemed like a challenge four hours ago was rapidly becoming a nightmarish setback.

Exercise 12: Team stress audit

TEAM SETBACKS

There may be little you can do to help a colleague going through a personal setback. However, as a manager you may be able to identify equivalent setbacks which your team may experience in the workplace.

What would constitute a setback for your team? It might include the following:

- Loss of team members
  - death
  - redundancy
  - retirement
  - promotion
  - pregnancy.

- A cut in resources
  - reduced budget
  - reduced staffing.

- Team split up
  - relocation
  - reorganization.

- A blow to morale
  - a team failure
  - external criticism
  - loss of business
  - bad publicity.

Which of the above have happened to your team? Can you think of any others?

Complete the stress audit again, this time focusing on your team. You may either try to produce a 'generic' audit for the whole team or, alternatively, use a separate sheet of paper and carry out the audit for each team member individually. Follow the instructions on the audit.

Make a note of the setbacks you think your team are facing. Try separating these setbacks into two distinct types: people- and task-related.

People-related
(for example illness, resignations, job losses, retirement, disciplinary problems, deaths, accidents)

_____

_____

_____

_____

_____

_____

Task-related
(for example lost contracts, failed projects, substantially increased workloads)

_____

_____

_____

_____

_____

_____

SKILLBUILDER

Environmental hassles

List the hassles your team regularly face in relation to their working environment.

Unfriendly physical features _____

_____

_____

Internal physiological states _____

_____

_____

Social contact _____

_____

_____

Travel _____

_____

_____

Information flow _____

_____

_____

Work pattern _____

_____

_____

Cultural hassles

Estimate the level of pressure created by the cultural hassles facing your team.

Mark the level (high, medium or low) for each issue and create your own team profile by linking the points.

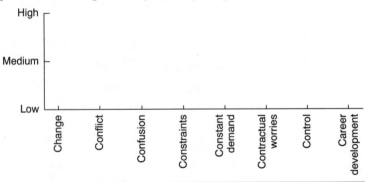

Challenges

List a range of challenges which are currently being faced by individuals or groups within your team.

_____

_____

_____

_____

_____

_____

Select one of the challenges above and analyze it using the four questions below. Be specific about what the likely sources of pressure are within this challenge.

The Challenge	
To what extent is it an emotional challenge?	Is there a physical element to the challenge?
Is it an intellectual challenge?	What meaning does the challenge have for us?

Overall pressure level

Position your team on the continuum line below taking into account all the setbacks, hassles and challenges they are facing.

Too low	Low	Optimal	High	Too high

NOW MOVE TO THE FAST TRACK SECTION ON THE FOLLOWING PAGE.

Generating audit questions

There are a variety of audit questions you might ask yourself or your team, on a regular basis, to help identify and control the build up of any pressures.

Here are some examples.

EXAMPLE AUDIT QUESTIONS

Setbacks
- Do I know which people have significant personal worries?
- Is anything happening at work which will be perceived as setbacks by team members?

Hassles – environmental
- What are the hassles in our working environment?
- What physical features might cause problems? (How comfortable are people?)
- Is the layout of the office a source of pressure – space, seating?
- Does the food and drink provision meet people's needs?
- Is travel to work or during work a particular problem for anyone?
- Is the level of information being dealt with by any individual excessively burdensome?
- Do the working hours give problems to anyone?

Hassles – cultural
- Which of the 8 Cs are inducing stress in our working culture?
- Are there any major changes going on?
- Are there any sources of conflict for anyone in the team?
- Is anyone under pressure through confusion over any issue?
- What factors constrain us from doing our job well?
- What are the demands on us?
- Are there contractual worries for anyone?
- Does anyone feel they are not in control?

Challenges
- What range of challenges is each person facing?
- Are their challenges too few or too many? Are they balanced?

- What is the potentially stressful area in any particular challenge?
- What is the significance of that challenge for them?

You will need to develop your own audit questions that are relevant to you, your work and your organization.

YOU MAY NOW CONTINUE WITH THE SKILLBUILDER EXERCISE ON THE FOLLOWING PAGE, OR MOVE TO THE NEXT FAST TRACK SECTION ON PAGE 91.

Exercise 13: Generating audit questions

Use our suggestions for audit questions as a starting point and write down **your own** set of questions. Bear in mind that you are designing a stress audit for your team. You need to make sure that the questions are relevant, relate to people's work and will be easily understood.

Auditing Stress Inducers in your Team			
	To ask an individual privately	To discuss with the team as a whole	For you to bear in mind personally
Questions on setbacks			
Questions on hassles			
Questions on challenges			

Learning Areas

In this unit you will:

- understand how stress can come from your own self-appraisal
- learn how to encourage helpful and positive thinking styles in your team
- plan actions to become aware of setbacks, reduce hassles and monitor challenges.

Appraising our own capability

The potential for stress comes from everyday situations that happen in our environment. These are what we interpret as setbacks, hassles and challenges. They present, however, only the potential for stress. Crucially it is the way that we think about those situations which will determine whether we actually become stressed.

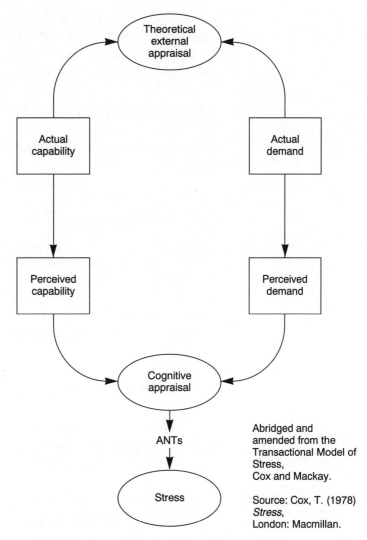

Abridged and amended from the Transactional Model of Stress, Cox and Mackay.

Source: Cox, T. (1978) *Stress*, London: Macmillan.

The Compound Model of Stress: Part 1

ACTUAL DEMAND

In any job or project there is real demand placed on the individual. This is the job or project description. It is what, in actuality, the job entails. It has outcomes and requires a particular set of activities.

ACTUAL CAPABILITY

A given person can be said to have an objective level of capability in terms of the skills they bring to achieve the job or project outcomes. This capability can be described in terms of an individual's education, training, motivation and experience.

THEORETICAL EXTERNAL APPRAISAL

A manager will naturally tend to match a given task to an individual based on their own appraisal of the demands of the work and the abilities of the individual.

PERCEIVED DEMAND

When we match a project to an individual, what is important is not just the actual demands of the work but the way the individual perceives those demands. It is their interpretation of the demands and what they think is being asked of them which is critical. Again the psychological meaning attached will be crucial.

PERCEIVED CAPABILITY

The individual's own view of how able they are to meet the perceived demands is also crucial. They may very well over-rate or under-rate their ability to meet expectations and to cope.

COGNITIVE APPRAISAL

This is the matching of perceived demand against perceived capability. Put simply, if people think they can cope then they are less likely to become stressed even where they do not meet the requirements and achieve the outcomes. Conversely if someone feels unable to meet the perceived demands facing them, irrespective of their real competencies, they are more likely to be prone to stress symptoms.

Each of the above is equally true for events unconnected with paid work. Consider, for example, someone who has three children, runs a household on a tight income and works part time. Suddenly that person finds him or herself faced with having to nurse a sick partner and asks the question, 'Can I meet the (perceived) demand?'

Automatic negative thoughts

Stress is likely to occur where perceived demand exceeds perceived capability for a sustained period of time because as part of this internal dialogue we begin to have automatic negative thoughts (ANTs).

These are unhelpful thoughts of which we are barely aware such as:

- 'I'm a failure, I'll lose my job.'
- 'I'm hopeless, nobody will love me.'
- 'I'm incompetent, I don't deserve happiness.'

These ANTs then provoke strong, negative emotions (and cortical arousal) unless challenged and countered with more positive ways of thinking. It is easy to suggest to someone who is feeling stress that they should think more positively but far less easy for the person involved to act on the advice. The next sections (pages 94–108) look at the role of the manager in promoting this positive outlook.

Despite the constructive advice Peter couldn't stop an unhelpful 'automatic negative thought' entering his head.

The mental style of copers

All of us cope with high levels of pressure at times. What is our mental style when we are coping? In other words how exactly are we thinking when we feel positive about the relationship between the perceived demand and our perceived capability?

Write two or three answers to each of the following questions.

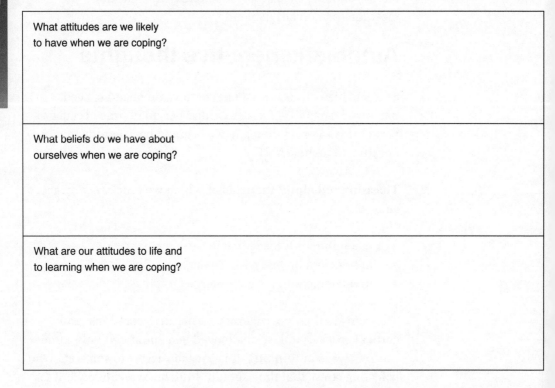

What attitudes are we likely
to have when we are coping?

What beliefs do we have about
ourselves when we are coping?

What are our attitudes to life and
to learning when we are coping?

The list you have generated is a description of the mental style of copers. It will probably include some of the following characteristics:

- a general mental well-being and sense of optimism
- the feeling of being in control
- a belief in your own competence
- the ability to focus and maintain attention
- a sense of perspective, separating yourself from your job performance
- a strong degree of self-knowledge
- feeling inspirational and creative
- the security of being part of a supportive team.

Encouraging helpful characteristics

These characteristics above are helpful in preventing an individual from becoming prone to stress.

Write two actions you could take (or do take) with your team in order to encourage each one.

Helpful Characteristics	Implications for Managers
A general mental well-being and sense of optimism	
The feeling of being in control	
A belief in your own competence	
The ability to focus and maintain attention	
A sense of perspective, separating yourself from your job performance	
A strong degree of self-knowledge	
Feeling inspirational and creative	
The security of being part of a supportive team	

YOU MAY NOW CONTINUE WITH THE SKILLBUILDER EXERCISE ON PAGE 97, OR MOVE TO THE NEXT FAST TRACK SECTION ON PAGE 101.

Exercise 14: Self-assessment

The following ideas for coping with pressure were all suggested by groups with whom we have worked.

- Make a note of any which you want to add to your own ideas
- Rate yourself on how effectively you promote each characteristic
- Record commitments you want to make in order to promote each characteristic.

Characteristic	Personal Rating	Commitments
1. A general mental well-being and sense of optimism • Talk to people and listen to what they have to say • Give good news to the team and take pride in the team's achievements • Smile at people/show them you care • Catch people doing things right • Involve others in planning • Make sure that an individual's workload is achievable	_____ _____ _____ _____ _____ _____	
2. The feeling of being in control • Delegate so people have a sense of ownership • Don't abdicate your own responsibility • Give people the authority they need • Make roles and responsibilities clear • Encourage active participation in appropriate decision making • Involve others in planning • Share information and ask people what they want	_____ _____ _____ _____ _____ _____ _____	

SKILLBUILDER

Characteristic	Personal Rating	Commitments
3. A belief in your own competence • Give a hearing to all ideas • Value all contributions in meetings • Provide challenges but do not over-challenge people • Motivate with praise which is clear and specific • Draw attention to past successes • Record people's successes • Promote lifetime learning	_____ _____ _____ _____ _____ _____ _____	
4. The ability to focus and maintain attention • Maintain a hassle-free working environment • Remove distractions in the workplace • Provide comfortable areas to concentrate • Identify people's preferred working conditions • Structure and time meetings carefully • Encourage people to take breaks from their work • Provide interesting, enjoyable and varied challenges • Make sure goals are clear with tangible milestones along the way	_____ _____ _____ _____ _____ _____ _____ _____	
5. A sense of perspective separating yourself from your job performance • Acknowledge other roles in people's lives • Do not have witch hunts but hunt for what we can do better • Give people physical and psychological space • Use distancing language and find out what, not who, went wrong • Recognize the achievements of people outside work	_____ _____ _____ _____ _____	

Characteristic	Personal Rating	Commitments
6. A strong degree of self-knowledge • Encourage reflection, debriefing and peer counselling • Provide opportunities for growth (diversity, training, promotion) • Ensure you have outside interests • Encourage stress management • Give clear affirmative feedback • Encourage personal development planning so individuals know their own skills and training needs • Demonstrate your own personal commitment	_____ _____ _____ _____ _____ _____ _____	
7. Feeling inspirational and creative • Tolerate half-formed ideas and hunches – build on them • Listen to ideas and encourage suggestions • Actively provide opportunities for creativity (time, humour, relaxation) • Encourage the use of initiative • Create a 'no blame' culture and a 'no fear' atmosphere • Look outside the company for themes and solutions (make connections)	_____ _____ _____ _____ _____ _____	
8. The security of being part of a supportive team • Swap compliments • Offer help to colleagues • Smile at people/show them you care • Involve others in planning • Promote social interaction and support people who arrange events • Take time away for team building	_____ _____ _____ _____ _____ _____	

SKILLBUILDER

It will be apparent that many of the approaches above are not exclusive to dealing with stress, they are principles of effective management. They are ways of behaving and managing the team that good managers have long since practised in order to ensure that everyone in the team feels fulfilled and is able to work to their full potential.

These same practices will help to prevent stress in your team.

NOW MOVE TO THE FAST TRACK SECTION ON THE FOLLOWING PAGE.

Tackling the causes of stress

The process of encouraging helpful mental characteristics will create a climate in which stress is less likely to occur in the team. However, this will not eradicate many of the causes of stress and it is important to recognize that as managers there are no easy solutions which can apply to all situations.

For any given situation we need to think about:

- our procedures and practices
- our style of management
- the way we work in teams.

It also helps to separate our thinking on setbacks, hassles and challenges. Clearly we have more influence over some than others.

A useful principle is to think in terms of:

- Being aware of setbacks
- Reducing hassles
- Monitoring challenges.

BEING AWARE OF SETBACKS

You are rarely in a position to intervene directly when team members are experiencing the type of personal difficulties or changes which we have called setbacks.

Your job as a manager is usually to 'be there for people' should they need your help in dealing with or talking through an issue.

Some useful questions to ask yourself are:

- Do I know if people are facing significant setbacks?
- Do I know which people want to talk through personal problems?
- Do I need to say anything?
- Is practical support required? (either job focused or welfare services)
- Would temporary changes at work ameliorate the problem?

Team setbacks

While there may be little you can do directly to help a team member through a personal setback you will have a central role in dealing with team setbacks. It is therefore important for you as a manager to consider how you respond to team setbacks.

REDUCING HASSLES

Whilst you may need to take the lead in monitoring challenges you may find that, using the activity below, the team as a whole is best placed to take the lead in reducing hassles.

GROUP ACTIVITY

ENVIRONMENTAL HASSLES

Step 1 At a team meeting or an away day describe to the team what we mean by hassles in our working environment, for example:

- unfriendly physical features
- internal physiological states
- social contact
- travel
- information flow
- work pattern.

Step 2 Divide the team into groups of two or three and ask them to identify about six main hassles in their working environment. List these on a flip chart.

Step 3 Ask each group to take one hassle and develop a plan of action to reduce its impact in the workplace. Get each group to report back and lead discussion.

GROUP
ACTIVITY

CULTURAL HASSLES

Step 1 At a team meeting or an away day describe to the team what we mean by hassles in our working culture.

Step 2 Draw the graph below on a white board. Ask people to consider what cultural hassles the team faces and what level of pressure they create.

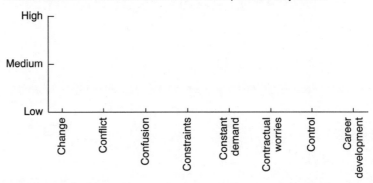

Step 3 Discuss as a team whether any of these cultural hassles can be reduced by either:

- improving the way we work as a team
- or by making specific recommendations to the organization.

MONITORING CHALLENGES

It is the manager's job to monitor the challenges facing members of the team. This will involve a general awareness of where each person is on their own pressure curve. Better quality managerial decisions can then be made when allocating activities.

You will find it helpful to build into your review process a section on the monitoring of challenges. Ask questions about the volume, nature and significance of challenges facing staff.

Such conversations will require a great deal of trust and openness between you and each member of the team. Long-term consideration needs to be given to how to encourage this.

YOU MAY NOW CONTINUE WITH THE SKILLBUILDER EXERCISE ON PAGE 105, OR MOVE TO THE NEXT FAST TRACK SECTION ON PAGE 113.

Team setbacks

What are the principles for you as a manager in helping the team to cope with a team setback?

- How should you behave?
- What should you do?

There is no simple answer to this but it seems that the following principles will be useful.

Communicate

Don't ignore the setback. Discuss it with the team collectively and individually if appropriate. Let them talk and listen to them. As with major personal setbacks it is important that people explore their feelings even if there are no simple solutions.

For certain types of team setback, such as a team failure, it will be useful to analyse the issue systematically so that you all understand it and learn how you might do things differently another time. Even here though it is important that the team do more of the talking than you do.

Support

The spirit and comradeship that you have built up over a long time are vital if the team are to feel supported by you and by each other. You will need to show sympathy to the team and to demonstrate how much you value them.

You may need to offer some practical support in finding a way through the setback.

Protect

When a team faces a setback, part of your role will be to protect them from some of the impact. You may need to convey to them that this is nobody's fault and not a reflection on their competence.

At times you may need to shield them from criticism by 'taking the flak' yourself.

Move on

Remember that it takes people time to get over a setback. Your role as manager is to judge the right moment to start to move on. You need to decide how to help the team to make sense of the setback and then to see the future as constructively as possible.

The example you set and the behaviour you yourself model will be all important. If you have been sucked into a cycle of despondency you can hardly expect your team to do otherwise. But be careful, your team will not respond to superficially positive behaviour which does not acknowledge the setback.

Your challenge is in managing the timing and balance of these principles according to your unique circumstances.

Exercise 15: Tackling the causes of stress

Use the questions below to help identify the actions you should take for tackling the causes of stress in your team.

Reducing hassles	
Produce a list of five typical hassles which face people in your team.	1. 2. 3. 4. 5.
What does it mean in practice to reduce these hassles?	
What is your role in reducing these hassles? – your practices, management style, team work.	
What audit questions should you constantly ask yourself?	

SKILLBUILDER

Monitoring challenges	
Produce a list of five typical challenges which face people in your team.	1. 2. 3. 4. 5.
What does it mean in practice to monitor these challenges?	
What is your role in monitoring these challenges? – your practices, management style, team work, supervision, appraisal, delegation, informal contact, and so on.	
What audit questions should you constantly ask yourself?	

NOW READ THE FAST TRACK SECTION AT THE START OF PART III (PAGE 113).

PART III

What are the Symptoms of Stress?

Learning Objectives

Part III will enable you to:

- understand and explain the symptoms of stress displayed within your team
- audit the symptoms of stress
- plan actions in response to the symptoms of stress you see.

The Symptoms

Learning Areas

In this unit you will:

- learn to recognize the physiological, emotional, cognitive and behavioural symptoms of stress
- understand why we experience these symptoms
- assess your personal experience of the symptoms.

Symptoms of stress analysis

The symptoms of stress can be divided into four broad categories. Read the descriptions below.

Physiological symptoms
These are changes in the functioning of our bodies and our physical reactions.

Emotional symptoms
These are changes in the way we feel about what is happening around us and how we respond in an emotional sense.

Cognitive symptoms
These are changes in the way we think about what is happening to us or in our style of thinking.

Behavioural symptoms
These are changes in the way we react and behave in response to the situations we face.

YOU MAY NOW CONTINUE WITH THE SKILLBUILDER EXERCISE ON PAGE 115, OR MOVE TO THE NEXT FAST TRACK SECTION ON PAGE 117.

113

Exercise 16: The four categories of stress symptoms

The following exercise will start you on the process of becoming skilled at identifying the symptoms of stress.

On the diagram below write down three key symptoms in each of the four categories which you would expect to see in someone suffering from stress.

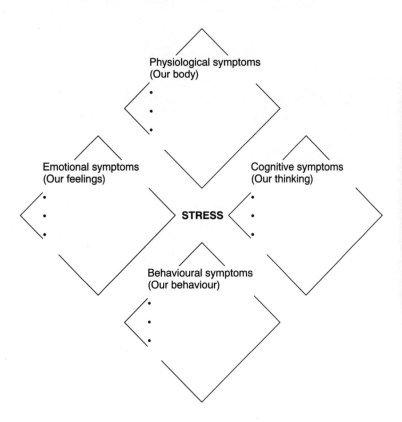

When you have completed the activity turn to the Fast Track section on page 117.

Why do we get symptoms of stress?

STRUCTURE OF THE BRAIN

In order to comprehend why becoming stressed involves unwanted and largely unpleasant symptoms, it is necessary to understand something about the brain.

The human brain has three major parts. In terms of its evolution the most primitive is the brain stem which is located at the point where the spinal cord joins the base of the brain. This is responsible for consciousness and general 'arousal' (or overall levels of brain activity). On the basis of information received through the senses the brain stem responds to environmental change by altering the level of chemical and electrical activity in the brain. In this way it acts as a sophisticated 'dimmer switch', attempting to match cognitive activity to external circumstances.

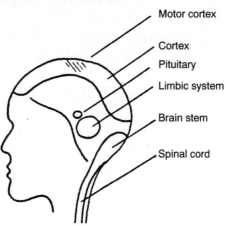

In the mid-brain is the limbic system where emotions are experienced, utilizing input from the brain stem and the cortex. The cortex is the largest and most evolved part of the human brain. It is where the high order thinking, planning and memorizing takes place.

LINK BETWEEN OUR MINDS AND BODIES

Increased cortical arousal is driven by the brain stem in response to environmental pressure/stimulation. This can be understood as an adaptive response to temporary demands or threatening circumstances. These can be either mental (excessive work loads) or physical (fatigue, heat, cold, and so on). The most widely known is the 'fight or flight' mechanism which provides an energetic drive in times of sudden danger.

The brain also produces changes in body functions via the autonomic nervous system and strong hormones affecting, for example, heart rate, breathing, blood circulation and blood composition. Part of the cortex known as the motor cortex also has direct control over movement and muscle tone.

MOVING FROM COPING WITH PRESSURE TO SUFFERING FROM STRESS

If environmental pressure persists the increased cortical arousal produces feelings of tension and eventually emotional states such as anger (based on noradrenalin) or fear and anxiety (based on adrenalin). At the same time changes in body function cease to be adaptive and become problematic. This combination of changing emotional states and body symptoms interacts with thought processes to produce the experience which we label as stress.

STRESS SYMPTOMS

In general a long-term stress episode is characterized by initial attempts to deal with the increased pressure/challenge by boosting arousal and hence alertness

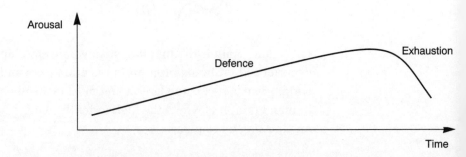

If the situation continues the defences become overwhelmed and arousal/alertness drops. This phase is characterized by withdrawal and fatigue leading to eventual exhaustion.

Personal checklist: The symptoms of stress

We will now look at each of the four categories of stress in more detail. After you have read the description record the symptoms you have personally experienced during a time when you were stressed.

PHYSIOLOGICAL SYMPTOMS

Many local physiological symptoms arise from a part of the brain known as the motor cortex which increases the neural stimulation to the muscles. This excessive stimulation often leads to tension, back pain, neck pain, headaches, nervous twitches and stuttering.

Other complaints can often be understood in terms of changes in hormone levels and these might include skin irritation, changes in heart rate and blood pressure, frequent urination and stomach upsets.

It is well documented that stress also depletes the body's immune (defence) system which results in a susceptibility to a range of everyday viruses and infections. Sufferers tend to feel generally 'run down' and prone to common colds and influenza. The link between stress and the immune system is by no means fully understood since, unlike all other body systems, there is no central controlling mechanism in the brain.

As well as these local, usually reversible, disturbances chronic (persistent) stress has been reliably linked to higher cancer rates which may be due to a long-term upset to the immune system.

Cardiovascular illnesses, which were once attributed to stress, are now better understood in terms of the physiological changes associated with intense and frequent anger. During an anger episode blood pressure and heart rate intensify but more significantly researchers believe that long-chain fatty acids are released into the blood to provide a rapid source of energy.

Whilst athletes may burn off this 'quick fuel' most people do not and over a lifetime this can lead to a harmful build up in major arteries.

Tick the symptoms you have experienced at a time of stress.

- Nail-biting
- Dry mouth
- Weight loss or gain
- Heart-pounding
- Dry skin
- Bruxism (teeth-grinding)
- Headache
- Clenched fists
- Increase or decrease in appetite

- Tight shoulders
- Frequent urination
- Diarrhoea or constipation
- Neck pain
- Stuttering
- Upset stomach
- Back pain
- Nervous twitch

A person suffering severe physiological symptoms will either be less effective in work or will be absent from work. The symptom rather than the underlying problem is likely to appear as the person's reason for absence.

EMOTIONAL SYMPTOMS

Anger is often used as a psychological 'defence' against anxiety and depression due to the attraction of its hormonal 'buzz' and energizing capacity.

Emotional defences are hard to sustain, however, and stress is characterized by a wide range of emotional symptoms such as mood swings, hostility, anxiety, apathy, withdrawal and feelings of hopelessness.

Tick the symptoms you have experienced at a time of stress.

- Mood swings
- Hostility
- Anxiety
- Insomnia
- Crying easily
- Apathy

- Depression
- Decreased sex drive
- Anger
- Hopelessness
- Fear
- Withdrawn

Not only do the emotional symptoms reduce our effectiveness but many of them make us difficult to work with and even more difficult to help.

COGNITIVE SYMPTOMS

Cognitive symptoms affect the way we think. In this domain symptoms result from our attempts to process information faster to keep abreast of increased task demand. Inevitably it becomes hard to sustain attention control and retain focus which is exacerbated by intrusive or irrelevant thoughts.

At this stage a person may attempt to reduce the amount of information to be dealt with by opting for a simplified belief system which denies the true complexity of the issues involved. Typically this might entail a move towards polarized problem-solving with a simplistic yes/no or right/wrong analysis.

This diminished judgement can involve an increased personalization of issues or a hostile egocentricity. In this case the sufferer can only see their limited viewpoint and begins to feel persecuted, interpreting neutral events as being directed at him or herself.

Lack of balance is completed by 'magnification' and 'minimization' whereby trivial issues are given undue emphasis whilst key factors are played down or ignored. This unsupportable level of cognition eventually leads to fatigue and a state of under-alertness characterized by forgetfulness, foggy thinking and disorganization which may be wrongly attributed to a lack of motivation.

Tick the symptoms you have experienced at a time of stress.

Over-alertness
- Anxious
- Unable to focus
- Intrusive thoughts

Under-alertness
- Foggy thinking
- Day-dreaming
- Prone to errors
- Disorganized
- Forgetfulness
- Decreased alertness

Distorted thinking
- Hostility
- Polarized thinking
- Personalization
- Minimization and magnification

It will be clear that over-alertness is our brain's valiant attempt to meet increasing demands and that under-alertness is the inevitable exhaustion which follows. Polarized or simplistic thinking is our brain's way of trying to save mental energy.

What should be significant for any organization is that individuals under stress produce a lower quality of thinking than normal.

BEHAVIOURAL SYMPTOMS

The fourth group of symptoms relates to aspects of behaviour. At first, increased arousal due to stress produces a sense of urgency and generally higher levels of activity, including talking too fast or too much, which can be unsettling for others.

There may be a heightened startle reaction and almost inevitably sleep disturbances. At this time sufferers also tend to lose their social interests, withdrawing from friends and family as well as neglecting stress-relieving hobbies. They may attempt to 'escape' by seeking comfort in food, gambling, smoking, alcohol or drugs which may help in soothing short-term feelings but soon complicate the original difficulties.

Tick the symptoms you have experienced at a time of stress.

Over-alertness
- Easily startled
- Sleeplessness
- Increased speed of talking

Under-alertness
- Decreased exercise
- Lack of social interest
- Withdrawal

Escapes
- Increased smoking
- Increased sugar or fat intake
- Increased alcohol and drug use

It will again be striking that over-alertness is our attempt to behave in a way which will meet the increasing demands on us. Similarly the stage of under-alertness is the exhaustion which follows. We also tend to exhibit distorted behaviour designed to make us feel temporarily better.

What should be significant for any organization is that individuals under stress behave in ways which are damaging to productive working relationships.

How do I know when a person is under stress?

It is very important not to overreact to the lists of symptoms you have recorded in the last section.

The facts spoke for themselves. Jane *had* put on 3 ounces. Weight gain *is* associated with stress yet instinctively the doctor sensed she was overreacting.

You will know if you have ever personally experienced even a relatively minor stress episode (and most of us have) that a number of the symptoms from each category are likely to be present at the same time.

The next unit of this Workbook will help you to audit the stress levels in your team with an intelligent eye.

Auditing the Symptoms of Stress

Learning Areas

In this unit you will:

- create an audit of the symptoms of stress in your team
- generate questions to help you in identifying the symptoms of stress in your team
- learn to assess when an individual has become stressed.

Symptoms audit

Now that you understand more about the symptoms of stress, the implication for you as a manager is that you will be better able to recognize the tell-tale signs that the stress level in your team or in individuals within it is beginning to rise.

You have to be careful not to place yourself in the position of playing the health care professional. However, there are probably some useful general questions which the manager may use as a private checklist when attempting to audit stress levels in the team.

TIP When you are trying to identify the symptoms of stress in yourself or those around you there are three important points you should understand.

First that you are looking for *changes* in normal physiology, emotional state, thinking approach and behaviours.

Second that you are looking for the development of a *number* of the symptoms occurring at the same time.

Third that most of your questions should be ones you would ask privately of yourself rather than putting them directly to individuals, though some may be ones that could usefully be discussed together by the whole team.

YOU MAY NOW CONTINUE WITH THE SKILLBUILDER EXERCISE ON PAGE 129, OR MOVE TO THE NEXT FAST TRACK SECTION ON PAGE 131.

127

Exercise 17: Symptoms questions

Below is a table showing the main physiological, emotional, cognitive and behavioural symptoms of stress. Generate two or three useful questions for each category to assess whether individuals are suffering a stress reaction.

STRESS AUDIT – Part Two: Symptoms

PHYSIOLOGICAL SYMPTOMS

- Nail-biting
- Dry mouth
- Weight loss or gain
- Heart-pounding
- Dry skin
- Bruxism (teeth-grinding)
- Headache
- Clenched fists
- Increase or decrease in appetite
- Tight shoulders
- Frequent urination
- Diarrhoea or constipation
- Neck pain
- Stuttering
- Upset stomach
- Back pain
- Nervous twitch

AUDIT QUESTIONS

_____

_____

_____

_____

_____

_____

_____

_____

_____

EMOTIONAL SYMPTOMS

- Mood swings
- Hostility
- Anxiety
- Insomnia
- Crying easily
- Apathy
- Depression
- Decreased sex drive
- Anger
- Hopelessness
- Fear
- Withdrawn

AUDIT QUESTIONS

_____

_____

_____

_____

_____

_____

_____

_____

STRESS AUDIT – Part Two: Symptoms

COGNITIVE SYMPTOMS	AUDIT QUESTIONS

Over-alertness
- Anxious
- Unable to focus
- Intrusive thoughts

Under-alertness
- Foggy thinking
- Day-dreaming
- Prone to errors
- Disorganized
- Forgetfulness
- Decreased alertness

Distorted thinking
- Hostility
- Polarized thinking
- Personalization
- Minimization and magnification

BEHAVIOURAL SYMPTOMS	AUDIT QUESTIONS

Over-alertness
- Easily startled
- Sleeplessness
- Increased speed of talking

Under-alertness
- Decreased exercise
- Lack of social interest
- Withdrawal

Escapes
- Increased smoking
- Increased sugar or fat intake
- Increased alcohol and drug use

SKILLBUILDER

NOW MOVE TO THE FAST TRACK SECTION ON THE FOLLOWING PAGE.

Suggestions for audit questions

It is important that you feel comfortable with the questions you develop. This is your stress audit and you should decide on your own list of questions which are useful to you and suit your particular situation.

The list below is neither a definitive nor a recommended list of questions. They are simply suggestions.

QUESTIONS ON PHYSIOLOGICAL SYMPTOMS

To consider privately
- Are any individuals taking increased and regular sick leave?
- Are increased numbers of people complaining of minor ailments?
- Are people missing out on lunch?
- Do I see changes in physiology and in health?
- Do I know individuals well enough to be able to detect changes in their health?

To discuss with the team
- Does the general well-being of our team seem to be changing for the worse?

QUESTIONS ON EMOTIONAL SYMPTOMS

To consider privately
- Are relationships in the office strained?
- Does the atmosphere in the office alter when a given individual is away?
- Do I sense an overwhelming mood of worry and depression?
- How much laughter and positive talk is there in the office?
- What does the body language in the office say to me?
- Has the mood among the staff significantly shifted for the worse?
- Is that person on an even keel emotionally?
- Are other people in the office hostile towards them?
- How am I feeling? Is this a barometer for what is going on?

To discuss with the team
- What is the emotional temperature in the office?

QUESTIONS ON COGNITIVE SYMPTOMS

To consider privately
- Is the quality of work being produced changing for the worse?
- Do people seem to be getting things out of proportion?
- How are people receiving constructive feedback?
- Am I seeing worrying changes in the quality of thinking in individuals?
- Are people finding it easy to focus on work?
- How would I describe that person's thinking?
- How open to others' ideas are we in meetings?

To discuss with the team
- How open to others' ideas are we in this team?
- Are we witnessing polarized arguments in meetings? Why?

QUESTIONS ON BEHAVIOURAL SYMPTOMS

To consider privately
- Has he/she become too quiet?
- What signs of over-alertness can I observe?
- Are people getting involved in staff socials as much as they used to do?
- What behaviour are we exhibiting in meetings?
- How is everyone behaving?
- Are people behaving differently?

To discuss with the team
- Are we rushing around more than we used to? Why?

When can I say it is stress?

The short answer is that you cannot be sure that a person is suffering the effects of stress and you are not qualified to do so. However, as a manager your responsibility is to monitor the performance of your team and you are entitled to observe behaviour, relationships and work output.

If you use common sense and good judgement when using the questions you have generated it will be clear if individuals are having problems.

It is important to restate that what you are looking for is a general increase in the number of possible symptoms rather than isolated examples of symptoms. One person suffering a stomach upset or making a silly error in their work probably means they have a bug in their digestive system or in their computer system, rather than that they are about to collapse with stress. Don't overreact!

As he called the emergency services the MD noted with quiet contentment that this was the 17th case of stress he had diagnosed this month. This time nail-biting had been the tell-tale sign.

TEMPORARY, SEVERE AND CHRONIC STRESS

Temporary stress
The person concerned is temporarily going though a period where they are under pressure. They are experiencing some difficulty in coping with this. They are at this point on the defence/exhaustion graph.

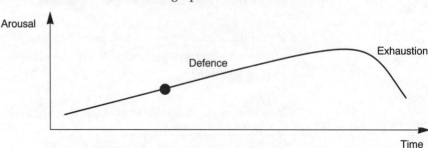

Severe stress
The pressure the person is experiencing is unusually high and has continued over a period of weeks. They are having great difficulty in coping with this. They are at this point on the defence/exhaustion graph.

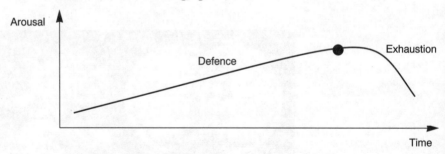

Chronic stress
The person has gone through a sustained period of great pressure from a number of sources and has effectively broken down and become ill. They are at this point on the defence/exhaustion graph.

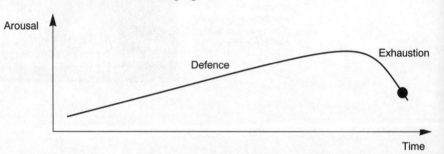

YOU MAY NOW CONTINUE WITH THE SKILLBUILDER EXERCISE ON THE FOLLOWING PAGE, OR MOVE TO THE NEXT FAST TRACK SECTION ON PAGE 139.

Exercise 18: Stress continuum line

On the continuum line below decide where you would place the people in the following four examples in terms of the extent to which you would say they were under stress?

Under pressure, not stress	Temporary stress	Severe stress	Chronic stress

EXAMPLE A

Two of Geoff's small project team, which installs new IT systems, have been off for some time leaving Geoff to manage a large workload with demanding clients virtually alone. The client has made a formal complaint to you about the quality of attention they are receiving from the company.

He is travelling a great deal and working long hours. He is losing his temper regularly in the office and picks fights with people in meetings especially those he considers have nothing better to do than discuss irrelevant long-term issues. He looks drained and anxious and complains of splitting headaches. He has stopped coming to the staff badminton evening.

When you raised the issue of the complaint he flew off the handle and stormed out of your office.

EXAMPLE B

Pamela has to make her first big presentation tomorrow on behalf of the borough council. She is very nervous and has not eaten all day.

She has lost her slides on the computer and needs to get someone from administration to do them for her. She is rushing around and biting her nails. When you spoke to her she said she hadn't slept properly for two nights.

EXAMPLE C

Frank is one of your senior sales managers. Like everyone he is having to meet increasingly tough targets in a very competitive market with reduced resources. The company has recently been taken over by a large American firm and there are great opportunities for successful and talented staff. Frank is certainly one of them.

You know that his children have recently left home and he and his wife have moved to a house in the country which they are renovating. They are coming up against all sorts of problems which some of the team are finding very amusing.

He seems to have lost his enthusiasm for work and is bitter and cynical about the likelihood of his strengths being recognized in the new company to the extent that he is poisoning the atmosphere. You are fairly sure he is drinking heavily and he has had several separate periods of 'food poisoning'.

EXAMPLE D

Elaine was a fit 23-year old until she developed a fairly serious back problem which may require an operation. She seems depressed and is no longer the life and soul of the office.

Before every appointment at the hospital she becomes agitated and her concentration on work suffers. She has stopped coming out with staff and always seems to have a chocolate bar at her desk.

NOW MOVE TO THE FAST TRACK SECTION AT THE START OF THE NEXT UNIT ON PAGE 139.

Learning Areas

In this unit you will:

- understand how stress affects an individual's capability
- recognize your role in breaking the vicious circle trapping the individual
- plan long-term preventative action to reduce stress in the team.

The effect on capability

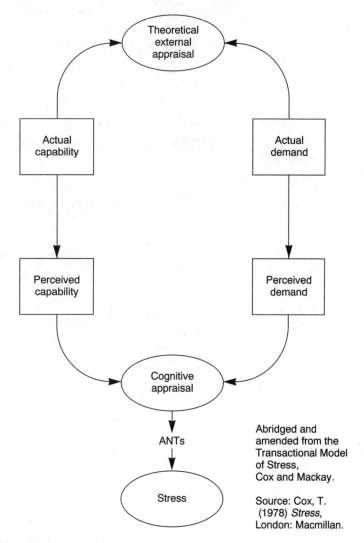

The Compound Model of Stress: Part 1

As we saw earlier in this Workbook, one crucial reason why a person suffers stress is when there is a gap between the individual's perception of the demands facing them and their perception of their own ability to cope which persists over time.

They make their own cognitive appraisal (mental comparison) and if there is a mismatch they are likely to produce ANTs and other symptoms of stress.

The following model can now be developed. It shows that once we are experiencing stress we also exhibit physiological, emotional, cognitive and behavioural symptoms.

Complete the diagram below with arrows indicating which of the categories of symptoms will worsen the person's *perception* of their ability to cope.

Now draw in arrows indicating which of the categories of symptoms will worsen the person's *actual* ability to cope.

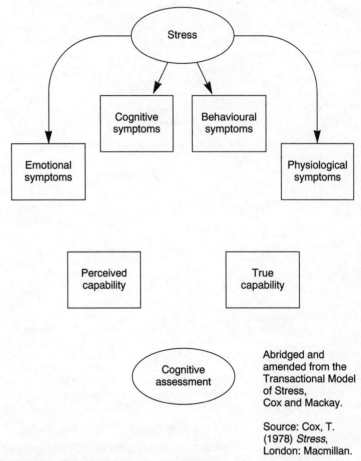

Abridged and amended from the Transactional Model of Stress, Cox and Mackay.

Source: Cox, T. (1978) *Stress*, London: Macmillan.

The Compound Model of Stress: Part 2 without arrows

What the completed model below reflects is that when we begin to experience the physical and emotional symptoms of stress they tend to lower our perception of our competence. Someone who is tired or run down is unlikely to feel in control.

A person who feels anxious or depressed is also going to experience a loss of self-esteem and confidence

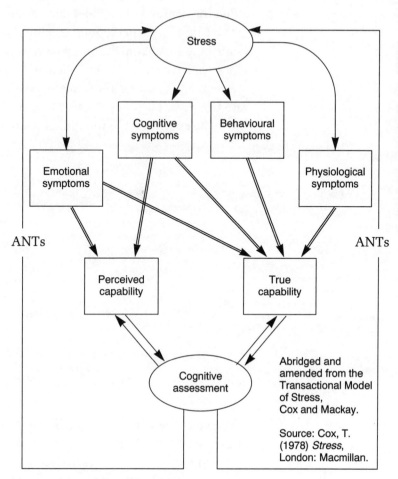

The Compound Model of Stress: Part 2 with arrows

Similarly some of the cognitive symptoms such as forgetfulness, inability to focus, intrusive thoughts and personalization may reduce our conviction that we are capable of performing well.

It should be clear by now that all four of the categories of symptoms are likely to affect our actual ability to do the job well.

Breaking the vicious circle

What the completed model demonstrates is that not only is stress caused by a perception gap but the symptoms themselves contribute to making the gap wider and the problem worse. Once we have started to experience the symptoms our subsequent cognitive assessment is likely to be more negative and the stress becomes worse. More symptoms develop and so the cycle continues compounding itself in a vicious circle.

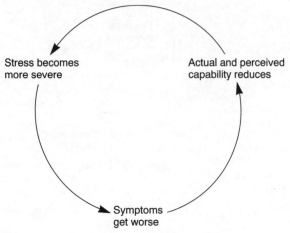

Stress becomes
more severe

Actual and perceived
capability reduces

Symptoms
get worse

Vicious circle

This is a circle which must be broken because stress is not an illness which might run its course and go away. It is our brain and body response to excessive environmental stimulation or pressure. Stress will not go away until the effects of those excessive pressures are removed and active intervention is needed in order to achieve this.

It is important to bear in mind that the sufferer is often in the worst position to make the necessary changes. Someone close to that person may need to step in to break the cycle. It may well be that a family, friends and peers can assist, especially if some of the causes lie outside work, but you as the manager are likely to be in an important position to help.

This may be difficult since the symptoms stressed people manifest can make them hard to help. If the person is withdrawn it will be difficult to assess the problem or the potential solutions. If the person is hostile they may try to push you away. If they are personalizing everything you can be sure they will personalize this. If they are angry, depressed or drunk they will not be very pleasant to be with.

In other words the symptoms might encourage you and everyone else to avoid them and their problems but it is likely they are ill-equipped to do anything constructive for themselves. Having said this, there are recurring examples of competent employees suddenly becoming ill with stress, without any obvious build-up of symptoms at work.

You as their manager are in an objective and influential position to facilitate another person's escape from the vicious circle.

What to do when you think a team member is experiencing severe stress

Before you do anything overtly you should step back and assess the situation.

- Audit the symptoms you feel the person is exhibiting. Can you see signs of a number of physiological, emotional, cognitive and behavioural symptoms?
- Try to decide what the inducers might be. Using your audit on team setbacks, hassles and challenges this will be relatively accurate. You may need to add some guess work for personal issues.
- Observe how other people in the team are reacting to the person.

Your next step will be to approach the person, preferably in a relaxed setting and in an informal way. Bear in mind that there are many barriers to someone accepting your offers of help. The symptoms of stress themselves may get in the way. A person who is distressed may be angry, resentful or dismissive with you. Other potential barriers include insensitive language, cultural misunderstandings, low levels of trust and psychological defences such as denial, or attributing the source of the problem elsewhere.

Once you are sitting down with the person one to one the golden rule, once again, is to listen to them. You need to understand what is happening before you can help. Also as one manager rather soberly put it 'you may be part of the problem yourself'.

The following page contains a list of some of the do's and don'ts of working with an individual.

TIP   **When working with an individual**

Do	Don't

• Prepare for the interview
   – clarify your thoughts
   – collate data if available
   – talk to a trusted colleague
   – give yourself enough time
	• Jump to conclusions
	• Ignore confidentiality
	• Deal with the issue 'on the hoof'

• Choose your words carefully
• Listen actively and patiently
   – nod and smile appropriately
   – show that you value the
     conversation
   – signal that you have allocated
     sufficient time
	• Cover up embarrassment with
	  inappropriate humour or excessive
	  formality
	• Be dismissive
	• Rush

• Try and disentangle the range of
  pressures from the symptoms of
  stress
   – attend to how it seems and
     feels to the other person
• Help to identify changes
	• Over-simplify
	• Impose your reality
	• Be fatalistic

• Encourage good stress
  inoculation practice
• Suggest ways of obtaining
  more support including
  professional support if
  appropriate
• Set a review date
	• Ignore the value of an all-round
	  approach
	• Forget about the whole episode
	  and move on to the next
	  problem

Having gathered more information a clearer picture will emerge of what you can and cannot help with. The person must play a key role in helping you to identify actions that you and other members of the team can take to support them. Such actions may include training, personal coaching or support, time off, flexitime, renegotiating objectives or deadlines and job redesign.

Where you feel the problem is serious or outside your control and you sense that the person needs specialist help, you should contact your own personnel department. They may take the problem away from you and if necessary suggest a doctor, counsellor, therapist, marriage guidance counsellor, debt adviser, bank manager or other specialist.

As with any work project you should monitor whether the course of action you are taking is working, review it periodically and reassess your strategy as necessary.

Throughout this process it is worth acknowledging the additional pressure you and the team are taking on. Talk with your manager. Do you need additional emotional or practical help yourself?

It occurred to the MD that he was developing an instinctive flair for this counselling business.

Long-term preventive action with the team

In the last section of this unit we looked at how to work with an individual to identify the causes of stress and the extent of their stress in terms of symptoms.

This, however, is very much secondary action because the problem has already started to affect the person. Let us think now about primary long-term preventive action.

YOU MAY NOW CONTINUE WITH THE SKILLBUILDER EXERCISE ON PAGE 149, OR MOVE TO THE NEXT FAST TRACK SECTION ON PAGE 151.

Exercise 19: Primary long-term preventive action

Consider what you have learned so far in this Workbook about what stress is, what causes it and what the symptoms are.

What long-term changes will help prevent your team becoming stressed?

At the start of this Workbook we asked you to think about your secrets of how to create effective team working. We suggested that a manager who follows the principles you set out will not only be managing well, they will also be preventing stress in their team.

Revisit your list of tools of effective team-building before starting the activity below. Which of those skills are you putting into practice well, and which ones need further work by you and the team to get them right?

SKILLBUILDER

Long-term changes which will help prevent your team becoming stressed

Make a decision now on which one of those areas you are
going to work on next and how you are going to do it. It may be
an issue for you as an individual or for the team as a whole.

Issue	Action

NOW READ THE FAST TRACK SECTION ON THE FOLLOWING PAGE TO SEE OUR
SUGGESTIONS.

SKILLBUILDER

Ideas for action

There are no right or wrong answers to the question of long-term actions. However, we do have the following suggestions.

- Review with the team how you set objectives for individuals and the team
  - how do we set objectives at the moment?
  - what works well in our current approach?
  - what does not work well?
  - how could we change our approach to reduce the stress objectives cause?

- Review with the team how delegation is working
  - what are the principles of effective delegation in our team?
  - are we living up to those principles at the moment?
  - what do we need to change to make delegation part of a programme of stress reduction?

- Plan a team-building event giving your facilitator time to talk to each individual privately before the event is planned using these questions:
  - what are the issues facing this team?
  - what causes you stress in this team?
  - what ways of working does this team have which work well for you?
  - what does not work well for you?

- Plan a programme of stress awareness for the whole team
  - If everyone understands what stress is, agrees its potential causes in the team, and is open about the symptoms then you will all be talking a common language which will make one-to-one or team discussions easier when they need to happen.
  - You could plan a day's event yourself using some of the team ideas in this Workbook; or you could use a professional in the area of stress; or you could add the issue of stress to the briefing you give your team-building facilitator.

The all-important question of course will be, having recognized the symptoms of stress and identified the causes, what can you do to relieve the situation?

That question is the subject of Part IV of this Workbook.

PART

IV

What can be Done to Reduce Stress?

Learning Objectives

Part IV will enable you to:

- understand and explain the holistic approach to reducing stress
- plan four strands of action for reducing stress
- apply your understanding to all aspects of your approach to management.

Learning Areas

In this unit you will:

- see how your learning so far forms part of the answer to stress
- receive an overview of how an all-round approach can reduce and prevent stress
- start creating an audit of what to keep and what to change to reduce stress.

The answer to stress

People often ask when starting a programme in stress management whether there is an answer, or some simple magical formula which will inoculate them against becoming stressed.

The answer is inevitably complex but there is an answer and it is contained in the acronym KARMA.

She wondered how she had ever managed before buying her new umbrella.

KARMA

In order to deal with stress successfully a holistic approach is required. Prevention is likely to be far more effective than cure. The first four of the following sections summarize work already covered in this Workbook. The last section, the 'all-round approach', will be developed as you work through Part IV of the programme.

KNOWLEDGE ABOUT THE NATURE OF STRESS

Prevention will come through an understanding of the nature of stress which leads to self-knowledge of our own pressure tolerance levels. If we understand when pressure becomes stress for ourselves we will be able to anticipate more successfully when that will happen for others around us. The battle is half won once you understand the enemy. It is important that the whole team, and not just you the manager, understands the issue.

AWARENESS OF THE SYMPTOMS

The process of sensitizing ourselves to those we work with is further aided by an awareness of the symptoms associated with stress. No single symptom should be taken in isolation, but cumulatively they will help us to detect growing levels of stress. If we become skilled at recognizing the symptoms we will spot them sooner rather than later. The result will be that the problems we have to deal with will not have reached such a serious state before we act.

REDUCTION OF CAUSES

Careful observation and analysis of our working environment, both human and physical, will enable us to identify the major stress inducers. It will also help us to isolate those areas on which we can have an impact and engage in reduction, monitoring and supporting activities in relation to setbacks, hassles and challenges as appropriate. This will help to create the climate where the manager can challenge the ANTs and promote positive thinking in the team.

MAINTENANCE OF EFFORTS

The holistic approach also recognizes the need for maintenance of our efforts. There are no simple one-off solutions which can be applied and immediately forgotten. Systematic vigilance is required together with a recognition that all the tools of effective management can also be stress inoculators when applied properly. For example, a manager who is a good listener and who is highly supportive will not only reap all the benefits associated with those qualities but will, at the same time, be reducing the likelihood of staff becoming stressed.

ALL-ROUND APPROACH

There are a number of tangible ways in which the individual can control rising levels of stress for themselves. These are the activities which are more popularly associated with the issue of 'dealing with stress'. Again it is important to recognize the holistic nature of these 'solutions'. No single action will prevent you ever experiencing stress. An all-round approach is required using a balance of these techniques if long-term benefit is to be derived.

The all-round approach can be summarized in four parts:
1. Promoting physical and mental well-being by eating sensibly, sleeping properly, exercising and indulging in hobbies and interests.
2. Obtaining support from a strong network of friends, family and colleagues.
3. Being assertive so that you know what you want and you can tell other people.
4. Giving importance to relaxation in whatever form is right for you.

A summary of these stress-controlling activities follows. They are intended to provide an overview only. There are specialists in each of these fields and an abundance of literature if you wish to examine any one approach in more depth.

Stress audit – Part Three: Interventions

So far we have audited the causes of stress in the environment in which your team works, and we have audited the symptoms the individuals within that team are likely to exhibit.

Now you need to audit the stress reduction activities that are currently in place. Develop a 'keep' list, that is, a list of positive actions that are already in place to protect yourself and your team from becoming stressed and that you should continue.

At the same time, start a 'change' list to record the number of small changes you could make to improve your protection. These lists will form the basis of your action plan for reducing stress.

It is important that your 'change' list consists of small, achievable actions. Very few people adhere to grand, life-changing strategies proposed in a moment of guilt or panic.

The All-round Approach

Learning Areas

In this unit you will:

- plan actions to improve the physical and mental well-being of your team
- plan actions to improve the support for members of your team
- plan actions to improve assertiveness within your team
- plan actions to prove the benefits of relaxation to your team.

Physical and mental well-being

Individuals who are mentally and physically in shape are better placed to withstand periods of pressure and are less likely to suffer from stress. Physical and mental well-being can be improved through regular exercise; indulging in hobbies and interests; getting sufficient sleep; and eating a healthy diet.

REGULAR EXERCISE

There are a number of benefits of regular exercise in terms of reducing the symptoms of stress.

Exercise reduces some of the physiological symptoms of stress by relieving the muscular tension which is caused by excessive signals from the motor cortex in response to environmental stimulation. Non-aggressive exercise lowers brain arousal levels in general because the brain is encouraged to shut out other stimuli during periods of engrossing physical activity.

Exercise also reduces the emotional symptoms since it leads to the release of endorphins. These are 'brain opiates' serving the emotional centre of the brain and have the effect of making us feel good thus countering to some extent the more negative emotions we may be experiencing.

During sport and exercise we aim to develop our competence and therefore tend to have a sense of control. This often extends beyond the physical skills level to the planning and social aspects.

Appropriate exercise also improves our self-esteem. Control and self-esteem are important characteristics of the mental style of people when they are coping. Exercise can improve the way we think and therefore reduce the cognitive symptoms of stress.

The development of self-esteem, the discipline of a fitness régime or sporting programme, the channelling of aggression and the social dimension of sport can all help to avert some of the behavioural symptoms of stress.

Finally, as well as ameliorating the symptoms, exercise is good for your general health and as such can counteract any suppression of the body's immune system.

INTERESTS AND HOBBIES

Having interests and hobbies outside of work provides pleasure which is helpful in countering the emotional symptoms of stress. They may reduce the physiological symptoms if your interest happens to be physical, for example, walking, digging an allotment, and so on.

The sense of self-esteem, perspective and control which your outside interests generate works in the same way as for exercise described above in controlling any unwanted cognitive and behavioural symptoms. This process is further enhanced if the interest involves good social relationships.

Where shared leisure activities take place at work, for example, in the company model aeroplane society or amateur dramatic group, they are likely to encourage the strong and more open relationships which are so vital for tacking problems together.

Hobbies are also likely to have an element of relaxation, the fourth strand in our all-round approach which will be discussed on page 191.

REGULAR AND SUFFICIENT SLEEP

Sleep is essential for our mental and physical alertness. It also gives us a sense of psychological well-being. The absence of good quality sleep will tend to exacerbate the physiological, emotional, cognitive and behavioural symptoms of stress.

Whist there is some variation in individual requirements it is particularly important for those who have irregular hours or who do shift work to take proper account of their sleep needs.

However, whereas it is within our control to change our habits in terms of exercise, interests and diet it is more difficult to change poor sleep patterns, especially since sleep is an early casualty of excessive pressure.

> **TIP** The following advice may be useful in overcoming sleep problems.
>
> **Planning**
> - Make sure you are getting enough exercise but don't take strenuous exercise, apart from sex, late at night.
> - Eat your meal earlier in the evening but don't go to bed hungry (milk and wheat in drinks are helpful).
> - Check temperature, noise, fabrics and mattress.
>
> **Routine**
> - If working late give yourself one hour to unwind.
> - Devise a pleasurable, gradual bedtime routine.
> - Progressively reduce electric light levels for the last two hours, if necessary ending with candle light (taking safety precautions).
> - Use music and simple relaxation techniques.
>
> **Avoid**
> - Do not use your bedroom for other activities, especially work.
> - Stimulation in the form of drinks (especially caffeine), films and music for the last two hours.
> - Negative self-talk, strong emotions and restlessness (easier said than done).
>
> **Suggestions**
> - If you don't fall asleep in 20 minutes or so, get out of bed and read in another room. Try not to associate your bed with sleeplessness.
> - Record the ideas you have during sleeplessness:
>   - capture the creativity
>   - put the ideas to bed (i.e. let go of them).

REGULAR AND BALANCED DIET

Much has been written on diet and will continue to be so. We will confine ourselves here to emphasizing that diet does have an effect on stress because it impacts on both our physiological and our psychological state.

> **TIP** **Experts agree that a good diet consists of:**
> - smaller and more frequent meals
> - a moderate protein intake
> - a moderate fat intake
> - maintaining a comfortable weight with no sudden dieting
> - a high carbohydrate intake
> - five fruits and vegetables per day
> - an adequate fluid intake including plenty of water

YOU MAY NOW CONTINUE WITH THE SKILLBUILDER EXERCISE ON PAGE 167, OR MOVE TO THE NEXT FAST TRACK SECTION ON PAGE 171.

Exercise 20(a): The healthy living working group

Let us suppose that your organization is run by a benevolent dictator. This managing director has decreed that the physical and mental well-being of everyone who works in the organization is a corporate responsibility.

A healthy living working group has been set up and you are on it. Your brief is to suggest a range of outrageous ideas for influencing the exercise, interests, sleep and diet of everyone.

In the space below brainstorm everything you can think of to influence these four areas. Record your ideas within the circle. Remember, this is a dictatorship so anything goes. Have fun!

ANSWER
BOX

We have had all sorts of wild suggestions from the groups we have worked with. When they are asked to translate these into potentially practical ideas it becomes clear that there is a usable theme in most of them.

Outrageous suggestion	Practical idea
Everyone forced by their manager to drink half a litre of water per hour	Cold water system in every office
All people failing the monthly test of running 3 miles in 20 minutes to be sacked	Voluntary health checks offered to all workers
Fines to be imposed on anyone caught eating chocolate at lunchtime	Free piece of fruit given with every meal in the canteen
Enforced sleep period from 1 – 2 p.m. every day	Silent reading and rest room available on site

Now go back to your creative suggestions and turn as many as you can into a practical idea which could be acted upon by your organization. Write them outside the circle connecting them to the wild idea to which they relate.

Exercise 20(b): Keep/Change audit, Part A

Study the first part of the keep/change audit below. Record all of the actions your team is currently doing right in terms of physical and mental well-being

KEEP/CHANGE AUDIT – Part A: Physical and Mental Well-being	
Keep	**Change**
• • • • •	

Review your list of practical ideas which have resulted from the outrageous suggestions. Choose at least one idea which you can commit to putting into action and record it in the 'Change' box.

GROUP ACTIVITY	You can use the process above as an activity with your team. **Step One** Prepare a short presentation for the team on the four aspects of physical and mental well-being – exercise, interests and hobbies, sleep and diet. **Step Two** Divide the team into groups of three and ask them to take part in the healthy living working group exercise. Explain it in the way it is explained in this Workbook. Take a presentation from each group on their outrageous suggestions. Have fun with it! **Step Three** As a whole group discussion, take the suggestions and agree what practical ideas can be derived from each of them. • Which are we doing already? • Which ones are possible in our organization? • Which single idea shall we act on immediately?

NOW MOVE TO THE FAST TRACK SECTION ON PAGE 171.

Obtaining support

THE SUPPORT NETWORK

A strong support network is essential to our well-being, especially in times of pressure. It will be clear as we consider different sources of support that no one person can provide us with all our needs for support.

Your close friend may listen to how you are feeling about work problems but only the building society can restructure your mortgage repayments. Your partner may encourage you over a particular challenge you are facing at work but only your manager can give you two days off to write that report.

EMOTIONAL SUPPORT

This support usually comes from family and friends. They listen to our concerns from our point of view. They are unequivocally on our side and provide us with safe refuge.

FINANCIAL SUPPORT

This support helps you to alleviate the pressure of financial burdens or the worry of them. It may come in the form of long-term advice or sympathetic short-term measures. This support often comes from professionals including financial advisers or bank managers and sometimes from our extended family.

PSYCHOLOGICAL SUPPORT

This involves three aspects:

- We get 'positive regard' from the listener
- We receive help in looking at a difficult issue from a different perspective or in a new way (cognitive reframing)
- We are encouraged towards 'positive self talk' which promotes optimism and confidence. This support may come from someone who is not personally very close to us.

POLITICAL SUPPORT

This comes from people who provide support for our ideas and aspirations. They will be people who are either like-minded or who are committed to the exploration of all views.

MANAGERIAL SUPPORT

As implied, this support is most likely to come from our manager or mentor in the organization. It helps us in the setting of objectives and agreeing of work schedules. Good managerial support helps us to review our performance positively and provides us with support in overcoming problems.

ORGANIZATIONAL SUPPORT

This support may well be anonymous. It is the support which is put in place by the organization such as the provision of positive reward and promotion structures. This support also comes in the form of the creation of an environment conducive to effective working including reasonable hours, adequate car parks and an appraisal system that works. An organization committed to auditing stress levels and reducing the causes would be providing good organizational support.

SPIRITUAL SUPPORT

This support comes from being part of a group with whom you share beliefs. It provides a sense of meaning and shared philosophy. Spiritual support may derive from membership of a local church or other religious community, though the same benefits can come from a political group, voluntary organization or pressure group.

YOU MAY NOW CONTINUE WITH THE SKILLBUILDER EXERCISE ON THE FOLLOWING PAGE, OR MOVE TO THE NEXT FAST TRACK SECTION ON PAGE 175.

Exercise 21: Your support network

As you read the notes on support construct a diagram of your personal support network on the chart below.

- Write the names of the people who fulfil each role
- Some people will appear more than once
- Some people will be potential rather than active members of your support network.

Support Network

Emotional   Financial

Political   Psychological

Organizational   Managerial

Spiritual

Exercise 22: Giving support

On the support network diagram below write the names of all the people who you think might put your name on their support network diagram. Include people from both your working life and your personal life.

Support Network
The people you support in different ways

Emotionally · Financially

Politically · Psychologically

Organizationally · Managerially

Spiritually

- Are there more or fewer people on this diagram than you would have thought?
- Do some colleagues simply look to you for managerial support while others look to you for more?
- Are there some names which appear several times because you fulfil more than one support role for them?
- How effectively are you supporting each of the people on the diagram?

NOW MOVE TO THE FAST TRACK SECTION ON THE FOLLOWING PAGE.

How to support others

The Health and Safety at Work Act talks of a 'duty of care' to colleagues. We would argue that as a manager you have a moral duty and a professional responsibility to support others.

Although we are generally in the best position to identify our own need for particular support, when we are under stress we tend to withdraw from social contact which can fragment our support network. Those around us may observe this happening and take steps to offer help even when it is not requested.

However, we will all recognize the fine line between concern and interference. The lesson for the manager is to create a climate within the team where individuals feel confident about seeking support and have enough trust in each other not to misinterpret that concern for interference.

It is unlikely that one person can meet all your needs for support and it follows that you, as manager, play only a part in the support network of others. If you understand what the support networks of individuals in your team look like you will be well placed to offer support which is appropriate and well received.

ACTIVITY **Personal affirmation**

You can work through this activity on your own. However, its real value will be in providing psychological support for a colleague. It builds confidence and self-esteem.

From the outset you should make it very clear that this process is completely confidential.

Step One: Record the successes
Think of two or three occasions when you have been successful either in your personal life or at work or both.

> *Examples*
> * Managed a large project team to implement new system of accounting
> * Organized the company family day
> * Supported a friend through a crisis.

Choose one of your examples and describe it in detail.

ACTIVITY   (When you are doing this with someone else you will have to ask lots of questions to get all the detail from them. Write down everything they say.)

Step Two: Extrapolate the qualities

Now extrapolate the skills and qualities which were required for each part of the success to happen.

Do this by asking questions such as:

- What skills did you need to achieve that part of this success?
- What did you need to learn?
- What were the difficulties you had to overcome on this?

As you ask these questions write down the skill or area of knowledge that you think you can infer from the experience.

> **Examples**
> - Got the best from the team and helped everyone to excel themselves
> - Fun-loving, great attention to detail, motivated people to give their time
> - Good listener, very patient, put my own priorities to one side.

Step Three: Write the personal affirmations

Go through the list of skills and qualities you have written down and check them out with the person you are working with. If they want to reject any as inappropriate they can do so.

Once you have agreed a list of qualities that they displayed during this particular success you need to convert them into a personal affirmation statement.

> **Examples**
> 'I am an enabler. People in the teams I lead give their best. They excel, they surprise themselves and they feel good about themselves.' – *The Accounts Project*.
>
> 'I am at my most successful when I make life fun for myself and others. I am effective in motivating others to get involved.' – *The Family Day*.
>
> 'People see me as a highly caring and selfless person who will put them first, support them and listen to them with patience.' – *Supporting my friend*.

You may write more than one personal affirmation. These can be written in your diary or kept somewhere else to refer to privately as an affirmation that you have a unique set of qualities which make you special, capable and valued.

YOU MAY NOW CONTINUE WITH THE SKILLBUILDER EXERCISE ON THE FOLLOWING PAGE, OR MOVE TO THE NEXT FAST TRACK SECTION ON PAGE 179.

Exercise 23: Keep/Change audit, Part B

Study Part B of your 'keep/change' stress audit below. Record all of the actions your team is currently doing right in terms of obtaining or giving support.

Decide on at least one idea for improving support within the team which you can commit to putting into action. Record it in the 'change' box.

KEEP/CHANGE AUDIT – Part B: Obtaining and Giving Support	
Keep	Change
• • • • •	

SKILLBUILDER

NOW MOVE TO THE FAST TRACK SECTION ON PAGE 179.

Assertiveness

If you work in an assertive environment where you and those around you are assertive, the whole team is less likely to experience stress.

DEFINING ASSERTIVENESS

Write words or phrases around each word on the diagram below to define what you understand by the words assertive, submissive and aggressive.

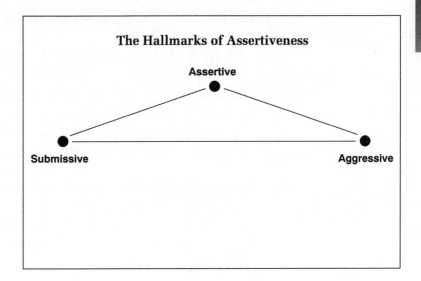

The Hallmarks of Assertiveness

Assertive

Submissive   Aggressive

CHARACTERISTICS OF ASSERTIVENESS

The main characteristics of assertive behaviour are:

- honesty
- clarity
- respect
- interactiveness.

Being assertive means being honest with yourself and with others. It means being clear in your own mind as to what you want and making this clear to others. It means understanding and respecting the position of others. It means being willing to listen to what they want and interacting with them to find win/win solutions to issues.

CHARACTERISTICS OF NON-ASSERTIVENESS

Non-assertiveness involves being either submissive or aggressive.

The main characteristics of non-assertive behaviour are:

- Resentment — harbouring or creating it
- Powerlessness — feeling powerless or abusing your power
- Embarrassment — feeling too embarrassed to act or causing it
- Stress — suffering or causing it
- Anger — privately feeling angry or using anger.

THE HALLMARKS OF ASSERTIVE BEHAVIOUR

Assertiveness is saying what you mean and meaning what you say. When you are not sure what you want from a situation it means being prepared to ask for time to consider the facts so that you are not rushed into making a poor decision.

Assertive people are not afraid to say 'No' and they find ways to say it firmly but without causing offence. They set clear limits from the beginning about the extent to which they are able to get involved in a project or any other sort of commitment.

Assertive people can give and accept compliments without embarrassment. They can also ask for help when they feel the need without any feelings of failure and they know that changing their mind is neither indecision nor lack of commitment. It is simply that they have changed their mind.

YOU MAY NOW CONTINUE WITH THE SKILLBUILDER EXERCISE ON THE FOLLOWING PAGE, OR MOVE TO THE NEXT FAST TRACK SECTION ON PAGE 185.

Exercise 24: Are you assertive?

Mark the position on the triangle which best describes your behaviour in each situation.

SITUATIONS

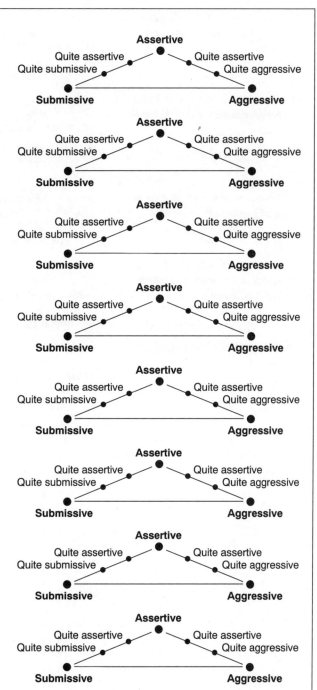

1. At a team meeting I am able to contribute my views even where I feel they may be unpopular

2. When a person asks to borrow something which I really do not want to lend them I refuse

3. When someone cuts in front of me in a queue I protest

4. When people talk aloud in a cinema, lecture or concert I am able to ask them to be quiet

5. When a shop assistant goes to a great deal of trouble to show merchandise I am still able to say 'no'

6. I am able to explain to my manager that I think there is a better way of tackling a piece of work

7. I would speak to my neighbours if their dog was keeping me awake at night

8. I accept compliments without embarrassment

9. When served food at a restaurant that is not prepared in the way I ordered it I express my dissatisfaction

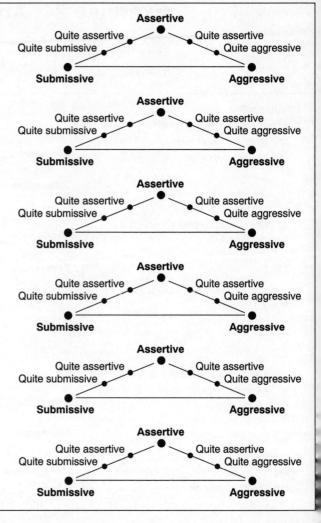

10. I would speak to my colleagues if their chatting was interrupting my work

11. When a friend offers an invitation I do not want to accept I can turn them down

12. When parents, in-laws or friends offer advice I express appreciation without feeling obliged to follow it

13. I would feel able to offer constructive advice to a colleague if I felt they had handled something badly

14. I tell my friends and colleagues what I like about them

Describe one situation where you tend to be submissive

Describe one situation where you tend to be aggressive

How assertive would you say that you are? Is your tendency towards being submissive or aggressive?

Most people find that there is considerable variation in their responses depending on the situation. They can be assertive in one situation but aggressive in another and submissive in yet another.

What situations in the workplace need more assertive behaviour than either you or your team are currently practising? In other words are there some situations in which you should be less submissive and others in which you should be less aggressive?

NOW MOVE TO THE FAST TRACK SECTION ON PAGE 185.

Implications for managers

The implications for managers are that they should understand assertiveness, be assertive and encourage it in others.

This involves:

- Deciding whether they behave sufficiently assertively in work situations
- Asking whether assertiveness is an issue in your team for you or for others
- Thinking about the extent to which you promote assertiveness within the team.

This Workbook does not attempt to include a full assertiveness training programme. However, the following advice may be useful in helping you to answer the question whether further work would be useful within your team since it provides a flavour of the content of an assertiveness programme.

Increasing assertiveness

TIP Your ability to be assertive will increase if you follow this three-part approach.

Step One – Decide
- Decide in detail what you want to happen
- Identify any uncertainties and irrational worries (i.e. barriers to action)
- Identify any areas where lack of self-esteem is holding you back.

Step Two – Plan
- Plan your script, writing it down if necessary
- Don't rely on flashes of inspiration but set your agenda from the start
- Take account of speech*, body language** and location.

Step Three – Act
- Reduce your anxiety by practising your script
- Sometimes a comforting personal affirmation, visual image or favourite object can help
- Celebrate your success!

*It is important to make your speech clear with simple messages. Keep your tone steady and if necessary repeat what you have to say like a 'broken record'. Try to use 'I' statements which focus on how you feel and what you have to say rather than 'You' statements which make assumptions about the other person's behaviour or motivation. These can cause offence and fuel argument.

**Assertive body language involves maintaining appropriate eye contact and an open posture which is friendly but confident. Stand if the other person is standing and sit if they are sitting. If someone is above you it is harder to be assertive. Get yourself anchored or planted so you feel sure of yourself.

Note
An assertiveness course would almost certainly identify real situations in which you act non-assertively and give you the opportunity to practise and receive feedback.

***GROUP
ACTIVITY***

Whole team discussion on assertiveness

Step One

Distribute copies of the diagram below and ask the team members individually
to write words or phrases to define what they understand by the terms
assertive, submissive and aggressive.

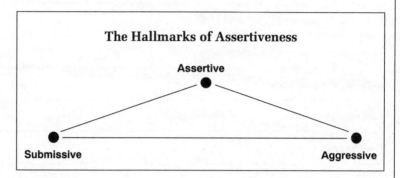

The Hallmarks of Assertiveness

Assertive

Submissive　　　　　　　　　　　　　　　　**Aggressive**

Step Two

Draw the diagram on a flip chart and ask everyone to call out their definitions of
each word. Discuss the definitions until you reach consensus.

Make a short presentation on the key characteristics of assertiveness based on
the notes in this Workbook.

Step Three

Ask the questions:
- What does assertiveness mean in our team?
- In what situations would greater assertiveness improve our performance?
- How can we improve it in our team?

ASSERTIVE BEHAVIOUR: a self-assessment questionnaire

Look at the hallmarks of assertive behaviour listed below. For each one rate yourself in terms of how consistently you practise the characteristic.

Characteristic	Rarely	Usually	Always
I say what I mean and I mean what I say			
I use 'I' statements not 'You' statements			
I say 'No' when necessary			
I set clear limits			
I ask for help			
I give and accept compliments			
I admit mistakes			
I apologize			
I ask for time to think things over			
I am prepared to go against the majority view			
I look for win/win outcomes			

YOU MAY NOW CONTINUE WITH THE SKILLBUILDER EXERCISE ON THE FOLLOWING PAGE, OR MOVE TO THE NEXT FAST TRACK SECTION ON PAGE 191.

Exercise 25: Keep/Change audit, Part C

Study Part C of your keep/change audit below. Record all of the actions your team is currently doing right in terms of being assertive and encouraging assertiveness from others.

Decide on at least one idea for improving assertiveness within the team which you can commit to putting into action. Record it in the 'change' box

KEEP/CHANGE AUDIT – Part C: Being Assertive	
Keep	**Change**
 • • • • • 	

SKILLBUILDER

Relaxation

The fourth strand in reducing stress is relaxation such as gardening, listening to music, progressive relaxation techniques and massage. Before reading on complete the following exercise.

Consider what you have learned about the nature of stress and what this Workbook says about the first strand in reducing stress, physical and mental well-being.

Write down three reasons why relaxation is likely to reduce stress.

-

-

-

WHY RELAXATION HELPS

Relaxation is an essential part of preventing stress reactions because in terms of our physiology it reduces cortical (brain) arousal and decreases muscle tension.

Relaxation also helps us to cope mentally as it distracts us and breaks into any cycle of worrying thoughts which we may be trapped in. Relaxation also provides us with a sense of perspective and encourages creative thinking.

EVERYDAY RELAXATION TECHNIQUES

There are many useful relaxation activities, all of which can help us both mentally and physiologically to a greater or lesser extent. These can be quite informal activities such as music, humour and pastimes including gardening, keeping pets, walking, taking saunas or swimming.

Throughout the day it is important to try and maintain a good posture, sitting or standing with a straight back, and with your feet firmly on the ground. Most of us feel early stress signs in one particular muscle group. It is therefore helpful to monitor our muscles for aches or tension and relieve them where necessary by gentle stretching.

We can relax our face by frowning and relaxing alternately; placing a warm towel over the face; or having a scalp massage or temple rub. Our jaw can be relaxed by placing the tongue on the roof of the mouth behind the front teeth. To relax our neck we can rotate it gently, and flex it by watching television on all fours or lying on our front. For the shoulders and back it is useful to shrug, shake and stretch.

Don't underestimate the importance of breathing steadily. Pressure may cause under- or over-breathing which can lead to anxiety or even panic attacks.

A simple way to relax is by 'just sitting'. In other words taking time out to sit quietly for a few minutes. Alternatively there are several techniques for 'moving slowly' which involve giving your total concentration to performing a set of simple movements as slowly as possible. T'ai Chi is a well-known example. Some people achieve a calming effect from 'witnessing' which involves regaining equilibrium by establishing a mental running commentary on your current thoughts and behaviour.

FORMAL RELAXATION TECHNIQUES

More formal relaxation can be practised through aromatherapy, involving perfumed oils. Massage is very popular. As well as traditional massage some practitioners offer a shorter, clothed version in the workplace. Reflexology entails massage to the soles of the feet whilst acupressure has similarities but involves a larger body area.

Most people are able to achieve 'progressive relaxation' and it is a common choice in ante-natal classes. This involves alternately contracting and relaxing muscles in sequence from head to toes. Many people find it a good way to get to sleep.

More formal still are relaxation through prayer; deep relaxation including hypnosis and guided visualization; and meditation including mind stilling and visualization.

Relaxation is a core aspect of stress inoculation and as such should be valued and the time protected.

Try to do the following
- Sit, stand and breathe correctly throughout the day
- Take sufficient breaks
- Establish a proper balance between work and home:
  - identify real working hours
  - try to avoid intrusive thoughts and phone calls
  - make good use of weekends and holidays
- Indulge in a range of simple relaxing activities
- Develop a more specific technique if necessary.

Implications for managers
- Office design should be functional but not exclude important social contact. This will promote mutual support and foster cross-fertilization of ideas.
- Consider how the architecture and interior design might calm and focus thinking. How about improving the view, redecoration, pictures, plants or even fish? Avoid sick building syndrome.
- Strike a balance between unhealthy lethargy and frantic or unnecessary activity. Ask people what feels best. Make sure office furniture is comfortable. Some big firms are introducing 'chill out' rooms with music and sofas.
- Are people taking proper breaks and holidays? Be aware of 'presenteeism' (are all those late nights really essential?) Who regularly takes work home and why?
- Show that you personally appreciate the need for relaxation.
- Support social activities engaged in by the team and encourage individuals who organize such activities.

YOU MAY NOW CONTINUE WITH THE SKILLBUILDER EXERCISE ON PAGE 195, OR MOVE TO 'EXTENDING YOUR KNOWLEDGE' ON PAGE 225.

193

Exercise 26: Keep/Change audit, Part D

Study Part D of your keep/change stress audit below. Record all of the actions you and your team are currently doing right in terms of encouraging relaxation.

Think about seating, break times, social activities and people who make the office fun. Do you give sufficient support? Do you help to find the time or resources for them?

Decide on at least one idea for improving relaxation within the team which you can commit to putting into action. Record it in the 'change' box.

KEEP/CHANGE AUDIT – Part D: Learning to Relax	
Keep	**Change**
•	
•	
•	
•	
•	

YOU MAY NOW CONTINUE WITH THE SKILLBUILDER EXERCISE ON PAGE 199, OR MOVE TO 'EXTENDING YOUR KNOWLEDGE' ON PAGE 225.

195

The Stress-free Office

Learning Areas

The final unit in this Workbook consists of a series of exercises to help you:

- understand how inoculating your team against stress connects to your wider management skills
- understand this connection in the context of two examples: setting objectives and listening
- make a commitment to your next steps.

Managing skills in the stress-free office

THE TOOLS OF EFFECTIVE MANAGEMENT

Return to the list of key management skills for creating effective team work which you constructed in Part I, Unit 1 of this Workbook (page 7).

Decide on no more than six of those skills which you would like to focus on here. Choose the ones which you feel are most likely to play a part in preventing stress in your team.

SKILLBUILDER

Exercise 27: The stress-free office

On the dart board chart below:

- Write the six key skills in the centre circle
- Unpack each skill in the second circle highlighting several particular aspects of the skill which are important if you are to put it into practice successfully
- Create a principle to live by based on this skill in order to create a stress-free office.

EXAMPLE

Key skill — Communication.

Aspects of skill — Listening, well chaired meetings, transparency and openness consultation, clarity.

Principle — We will create an environment where meetings and other settings for communication allow everyone to be heard; where there are no hidden agendas; and where everyone feels informed and clear about what is going on.

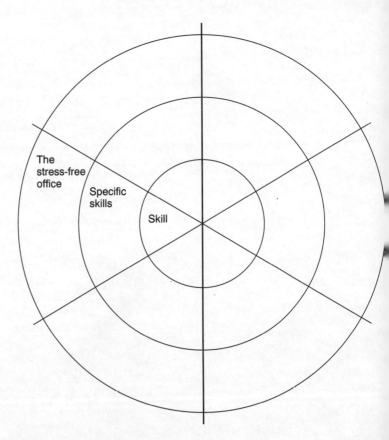

The writers of this Workbook cannot create these skills for you. They should be yours and written in a way which has tangible meaning for you.

In the next two exercises we will refer to two tools of effective management which, if handled well, will reduce stress. If they are handled badly of course the reverse is likely to happen.

These exercises will give you ideas on a structure for looking at some of the other issues which you have highlighted. They also provide ideas on how to approach discussion of such issues with your team.

SKILLBUILDER

Exercise 28: Setting objectives

We will start with objective setting. A major source of stress in organizations is having objectives which are perceived as:

- unrealistic
- too numerous
- irrelevant
- unconnected to real work.

EXAMPLE

A cartoon earlier in this Workbook (page 26) referred to a large company we worked with which had the system where line managers set objectives without consultation. Each line manager approached objective setting very differently but one middle manager complained:

'I'm incredibly overworked but I have just about got time to do everything I have to do but it's impossible to find time to do my objectives. I sat down the other day to do some of them but then something else came up and I had to leave them. And I've got 106 to do! All my objectives do is make me stressed out.'

It is therefore worth considering effective objective setting as a technique for reducing stress. We do not intend to give a full course on objective setting here though such a course may be something you wish to consider for you or your team. You might want to refer to the Gower Management Workbook, *Managing Performance* (Jenny Hill, 1997).

Start the exercise by considering the characteristics of objective setting within your team. On the chart opposite write words and phrases in answer to the questions posed.

Do not spend long on this. We want you to respond with gut reactions. The words and phrases you use will describe the characteristics of the way objectives are set in your team and in the organization.

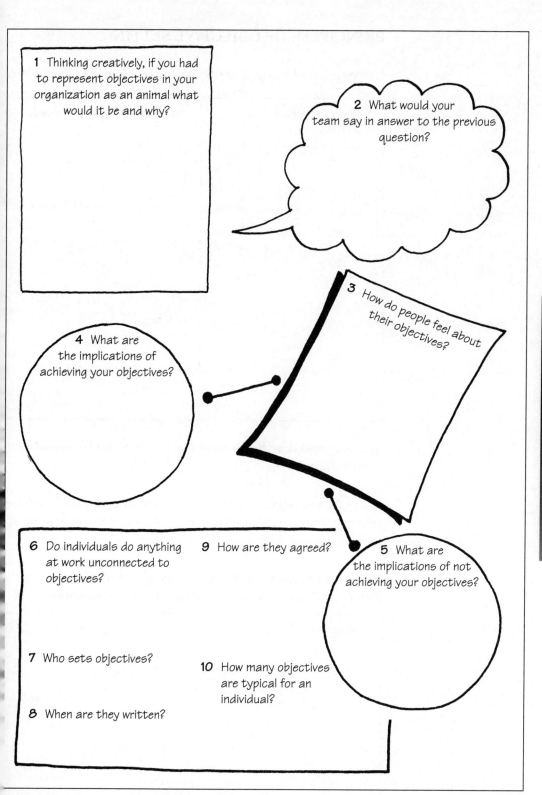

1 Thinking creatively, if you had to represent objectives in your organization as an animal what would it be and why?

2 What would your team say in answer to the previous question?

3 How do people feel about their objectives?

4 What are the implications of achieving your objectives?

6 Do individuals do anything at work unconnected to objectives?

9 How are they agreed?

5 What are the implications of not achieving your objectives?

7 Who sets objectives?

10 How many objectives are typical for an individual?

8 When are they written?

The characteristics of objective setting

PRINCIPLES OF OBJECTIVE SETTING

Use your list of words and phrases to complete the table below.

What are the characteristics of good objective setting?	What are the things to be avoided?
•	•
•	•
•	•
•	•
•	•

You may find that the 'things to be avoided' can be turned into positive principles.

Now that you have created the characteristics of good objective setting give yourself a rating from 1 to 5 on how well you meet each of these characteristics.

What commitments, if any, do you need to make in order to improve the way you set objectives? Record these below.

Commitments

You may want to transfer this to your dart board diagram at the start of this unit (page 200).

GROUP ACTIVITY

Repeat this activity with your team in order to improve the way objectives are set within the team.

Step One Ask everyone individually to complete the objective setting activity sheet. Share, record and discuss your answers.

Step Two Construct a list on a flip chart of the characteristics of good objective setting and the things to be avoided.

Step Three Discuss how you measure up as a team and agree any necessary commitments to improving your approach.

SKILLBUILDER

Exercise 29: The role of listening

INTRODUCTION

You will probably be familiar with the saying that we have two ears and one mouth and that we should use them in that proportion. It is sound advice. Effective listening is the essential core of good working relationships (and indeed all relationships).

EXAMPLE

In our work we have heard all too often people complaining about the extent to which they are listened to. The following example is typical.

'The management always go through a long consultation exercise and then they do what they planned to do in the first place.'

Start the exercise by reviewing the programme in this Workbook and answering the following questions.

Question	Answer
1. How will listening contribute to recognizing if people in the team are under stress?	
2. How will listening help us to identify the potential sources of stress in the team?	
3. How will listening help us to spot the symptoms of stress in others early?	
4. How will listening enable us to develop plans of action for reducing stress in the team?	

It will probably be clear from your answers that the manager, however insightful and intuitive, cannot answer these questions alone. In order to understand if stress is an issue, what is causing it, who is suffering from it and how to deal with it, the involvement of everyone is essential.

We need to listen carefully to the people we work with to understand their feelings, perspectives, needs and ideas.

You may also have observed that a lack of listening may itself be a source of stress particularly in relation to the cultural environment in which we work. When we are not being listened to we tend to feel undervalued and uninvolved.

SKILLBUILDER

Exercise 30: What is good listening?

Write words and phrases around the figure below which describe the specific skills of good listeners.

The following questions may stimulate your thinking:

- Think of someone you know to be a good listener – what do they do?
- Think of someone who is not a good listener – what is it they are not doing?
- What do good listeners say?
- What is their body language like?
- What do they do while you are talking?
- What are the attitudes and beliefs of good listeners?
- How do good listeners get you to talk?

Write below a principle to live by based on the skill of listening in order to create a stress-free office.

You may want to transfer this to your dart board diagram at the start of this unit (page 200).

Exercise 31: Self-assessment

From the previous exercise choose six characteristics of
effective listening. Write them in the left-hand column below.
In the second column give yourself a rating of 1 to 5 on how
well you practise these characteristics. In the third column rate
the team as a whole from 1 to 5 on how far it displays the
characteristics of effective listening.

Characteristic	Self-assessment	Team assessment

What commitments if any do you and/or the team need to
make in order to improve the way you listen? Record these
below.

Commitments

SKILLBUILDER

GROUP ACTIVITY

Repeat these activities with your team in order to improve the way you listen within the team.

Step One Use your ideas from the first activity in this section to explain how improved listening in the team will help to identify the causes, symptoms and solutions to stress within the team.

Step Two Use the 'what is good listening' activity with the whole team to produce a list of characteristics of effective listening which everyone can agree on.

Step Three Discuss how you measure up as a team and agree any necessary commitments to improve your approach.

Exercise 32: Personal commitments

Before you put this Workbook down review the sections where you have recorded ideas for preventing or reducing stress in your team.

Record below at least three personal commitments to improving or developing your style of management.

Personal commitments

211

Exercise 33: Practical actions

Record below three practical actions you intend to take in order to reduce stress in your team.

These may include:

- Personal actions as the manager
- Awareness-raising discussions with the team
- Team development programmes on specific issues such as 'assertiveness'
- Team discussions to identify the causes of stress
- Processes for monitoring stress levels
- Implementing ideas for dealing with stress.

Practical actions

SKILLBUILDER

Exercise 34: Trapped in a lift

Imagine for a moment that you have found yourself trapped in a lift between floors with a number of other people. You have been there for over two hours already.

The MD was delighted. At last the chance to test his new knowledge in the field.

Use the knowledge you have acquired using this Workbook to analyse what is happening.

DEFINITION

Look at your definition of stress in Part I, Unit 2 (page 29). Could what is happening in the lift be described as stressful according to your definition?

CAUSES

Remind yourself of the causes of stress in Part II, Unit 1, particularly the hassles (page 51). What are the major factors which are making this situation stressful?

SYMPTOMS

Remind yourself of the symptoms of stress in Part III, Unit 1 (page 113). What are the range of short-term symptoms being exhibited in the lift?

DEALING WITH STRESS

Remind yourself of the all-round approach for dealing with stress in Part IV, Unit 2 (page 159). Assuming you are not going to be released for some hours what could you do to reduce the level of stress in the lift?

SKILLBUILDER

Your analysis will have told you that this is a stressful situation for a variety of reasons. It represents a dramatic, unwanted change placing you in a threatening situation over which you have little control. Temperature, light and ventilation cannot be modified. You have no access to drink, food or toilets, and you are in too close proximity to others.

People will react in different ways. You will see physiological symptoms such as sweating, trembling or nail-biting. You will also be aware of a range of emotions from anxiety to anger and cognitive symptoms such as magnification or personalization. There are likely to be various behavioural symptoms from increased speed of talking to withdrawal.

Your analysis will also have told you that there are ways of reducing the stress such as optimistic talk; keeping a sense of perspective; distracting everyone with some sort of game; offering emotional support to people who need it; and finding ways to relax.

Of course, if you suddenly remembered that you had a box of chocolates in your bag the effect of handing them out would have an immediate therapeutic, if temporary, effect. (Apart from tasting good, the combination of fat and sugar produces a brief increase in a pleasurable brain chemical, serotonin.)

If there is one piece of advice the authors of this Workbook would like to offer it is to make sure that you always take a box of chocolates with you when you step into a lift.

Stress audit

The following is a complete stress audit based on the three separate sections developed in the Workbook.

STRESS AUDIT – Part One: Inducers

SECTION ONE: SETBACKS

Make a list of the setbacks you are currently facing or have faced in the last 12 months.

_____

_____

_____

_____

_____

_____

_____

_____

_____

_____

SECTION TWO: HASSLES

Environmental hassles

List the hassles you regularly face in relation to your working environment under the given headings.

Unfriendly physical features   _____

_____

Internal physiological states   _____

_____

Social contact   _____

_____

Travel   _____

_____

Information flow   _____

_____

Work pattern   _____

_____

STRESS AUDIT – Part One (continued)

Now record the level of pressure created by the cultural hassles you face. Mark the level (high, medium or low) for each issue and create your own graph by linking the points.

Cultural hassles
Record level of pressure created by the cultural hassles you face.

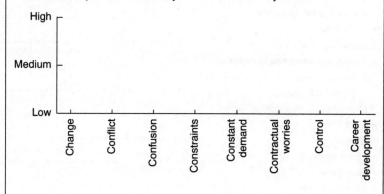

SECTION THREE: CHALLENGES

Challenges _____   _____

_____   _____

_____   _____

Overall pressure level
Position yourself on the continuum line below taking into account all the setbacks, hassles and challenges you are facing. We suggest you return to this three or four times over a couple of days to produce an average estimate.

Too low	Low	Optimal	High	Too high

STRESS AUDIT – Part Two: Symptoms

PHYSIOLOGICAL SYMPTOMS

- Nail-biting
- Dry mouth
- Weight loss or gain
- Heart-pounding
- Dry skin
- Bruxism (teeth-grinding)
- Headache
- Clenched fists
- Increase or decrease in appetite
- Tight shoulders
- Frequent urination
- Diarrhoea or constipation
- Neck pain
- Stuttering
- Upset stomach
- Back pain
- Nervous twitch

AUDIT QUESTIONS

_____

_____

_____

_____

_____

_____

_____

_____

_____

EMOTIONAL SYMPTOMS

- Mood swings
- Hostility
- Anxiety
- Insomnia
- Crying easily
- Apathy
- Depression
- Decreased sex drive
- Anger
- Hopelessness
- Fear
- Withdrawn

AUDIT QUESTIONS

_____

_____

_____

_____

_____

_____

_____

_____

_____

_____

_____

STRESS AUDIT – Part Two (continued)

COGNITIVE SYMPTOMS   **AUDIT QUESTIONS**

Over-alertness
- Anxious   _____
- Unable to focus   _____
- Intrusive thoughts   _____

Under-alertness   _____
- Foggy thinking   _____
- Day-dreaming   _____
- Prone to errors   _____
- Disorganized   _____
- Forgetfulness   _____
- Decreased alertness   _____

Distorted thinking   _____
- Hostility   _____
- Polarized thinking   _____
- Personalization   _____
- Minimization and magnification   _____

BEHAVIOURAL SYMPTOMS   **AUDIT QUESTIONS**

Over-alertness
- Easily startled   _____
- Sleeplessness   _____
- Increased speed of talking   _____

Under-alertness   _____
- Decreased exercise   _____
- Lack of social interest   _____
- Withdrawal   _____

Escapes   _____
- Increased smoking   _____
- Increased sugar or fat intake   _____
- Increased alcohol and drug use   _____

_____

_____

KEEP/CHANGE AUDIT – Part A: Physical and Mental Well-being

Keep	Change
•	
•	
•	
•	
•	

KEEP/CHANGE AUDIT – Part B: Obtaining and Giving Support

Keep	Change
•	
•	
•	
•	
•	

KEEP/CHANGE AUDIT – Part C: Being Assertive

Keep	Change
•	
•	
•	
•	
•	

KEEP/CHANGE AUDIT – Part D: Learning to Relax	
Keep	**Change**
• • • • •	

Extending your Knowledge

COURSES

Managing the Stress-free Office
Jim Welch Training and Development
88 Southgrove Road, Sheffield S10 2NQ
Tel.: 0114 267 8746

BOOKS

on stress

Stress and Employer Liability
by Jill Earnshaw and Cary Cooper, IPD.

Managing Pressure for Peak Performance
by Stephen Williams, Kogan Page.

Handbook on Stress, Medicine and Health
by Cary Cooper, Bota Rotan, Florida.

on personal effectiveness

Feel the Fear and Do It Anyway
by Susan Jeffers, Arrow.

Managing Performance
by Jenny Hill, Gower.

The 10 Natural Laws of Successful Time Management: Power Strategies for Increased Productivity and Inner Peace
by H.W. Smith, Nicholas Brealey Publishing.

The Seven Habits of Highly Effective People
by Stephen R. Covey, Simon & Schuster.

ORGANIZATIONS

International Stress Management Association (UK)
South Bank University, LP55
103 Borough Road, London SE1 0AA

Institute of Personnel and Development
IPD House, Camp Road, Wimbledon, London SW19 4UX

VIDEOS

Stress
Thirty minutes. Aimed at those responsible for coping with
stress in others.
CTVC Film Library
Hillside, Merry Hill Road, Bushey, Herts WD2 1DR
Tel.: 0181 950 4426

Stress at Work
British Medical Association
Film Library
BMA House, Tavistock Square, London WC1H 9JP
Tel.: 0171 388 7976

Managing Information

Working Smarter Not Harder

Hugh Garai

A Gower Management Workbook

Managing Information is based on a radical approach to the handling of information, where success goes to those who 'work smarter, not harder'. From it you will learn how to survive and thrive under incessant bombardment from data of every conceivable kind.

The Workbook will show you how to achieve more by doing less, and introduce you to ways of thinking and acting that will help you create a new framework for information handling. With the aid of examples, tips and exercises, you can make sure that you become a beneficiary of the IT revolution rather than one of its victims.

Gower

Managing People

Jane Churchouse and Chris Churchouse

A Gower Management Workbook

Good people managers are proactive; they use a mix of techniques including careful planning, good communication and adequate monitoring and support to ensure that, whilst they can handle the crises, they can also help their people move forward on a day-to-day basis.

This Workbook - part of the the Gower Management Workbook series - opens with a situation that every manager will undoubtedly face on a number of occasions: a key member of staff is leaving. The authors then provide a mix of theory and practice, case studies and exercises that will help any manager identify how to learn from the loss of a staff member; recruit a replacement and ensure that, from Day One, you manage and develop them in a way that will enable them to become a highly effective team member who can grow and develop within your organization.

Written for first and second-line managers, the Workbook is based around Level 4 of the latest MCI Management Standards. The relevant advice and techniques along, with the developmental exercises, provide the reader with an interactive and absorbing way of improving both their immediate and longer term performance - and that of the people that they manage.

Gower

Managing Performance

Goals, Feedback, Coaching, Recognition

Jenny Hill

A Gower Management Workbook

Managing Performance shows how you can make dramatic improvements in the workplace by focusing on four key elements: objectives, coaching, feedback and recognition. First, it will help you set clear objectives for yourself and your team. Next, it provides a simple seven-step coaching plan. Then you will learn powerful techniques for giving feedback to reinforce success. Finally, you will master the art of recognizing and rewarding performance, perhaps the most powerful weapon in the motivational armoury.

Gower

Team Leadership

Five Interactive Management Adventures

Graham Kelly

Managers have had *adventures* in their working lives ever since work became organized, and the shift towards teamworking has only served to add to their complexity. Underperforming team members, inappropriate behaviour or conflict within the team, poor communication – the list is endless.

Decisions have to be taken on the basis of what you know, what you assume and what you can guess.

Team Leadership captures something of these *adventures*. It gives you, 'the management adventurer', the opportunity to assess situations, evaluate options and their associated risks, and then to make a decision and see the outcome - all without affecting your career!

At each stage along the way, you'll be put on the spot to explain your decisions ... to test yourself as a management adventurer. Are you sharp enough to cope with these tricky scenarios? Can you analyse and understand the situations in which you find yourself? Can you evaluate the options facing you and assess the likely consequences and risks involved? Can you really take decisions and live them sufficiently to make them stick?

While team leadership can be real, serious stuff, this book proves that your personal and professional development can also be fun.

Gower

Training and Developing Your Team

John Humphries

A Gower Management Workbook

Managers come in all shapes and sizes, from differing backgrounds and disciplines and with a variety of skills and abilities. Exactly the same is true of the people that they manage. Which can make the responsibility a manager carries for training and developing their team a real challenge.

But there are plenty of opportunities and different techniques that are open to you for helping the individuals for whom you are responsible, to develop their skills, to learn new techniques and to embrace new attitudes towards the way that they work. John Humphries' Workbook will help you acquire the understanding and skills to exploit these opportunities and use these techniques, at your own pace. Using a mix of facts, techniques, questionnaires, exercises and projects, it provides you with the means to:

- understand the full range of opportunities and techniques open to you
- discover what kind of training and development your people need
- decide when to intervene and how to involve individuals in their own development strategy
- design and deliver simple training courses
- make use of techniques such as delegation, coaching, and involvement
- record and evaluate what you have done.

Gower